Overtures to Motion

Albert Drake

Acknowledgements

The following essays first appeared, often in different form, in *Old Cars Weekly*:

"The Atomic Age", "Baked Enamel", "The Beautiful and the Banal", "Clarence Young's *Motor Boys* had Grit", "Colorful Hues of '50s Not Only on Cars", "The Fisher Body Craftsman Guild Competition", "*Foto Review*", "The Home Front", "Hulks", "A Mechanic's Primer", "Memories of the World, Circa 1941", "Mid-Depression Packard", "The Mile-O-Meter", "A Nearly-Modern Story Book", "That 1941 Chevy Meant Something to Mom", "1951 Daytona Beach Trials, or How Fast was that Nash?", "1953 Cadillac Le Mans", "1942 Mercury", "Oasis", "Painting White Sidewall Tires", "The Present Refused", "Rationing", "'Sell 'N 'Swap' Magazine Ads", "The Sidewalk Flyer", "A Simplimatic Time", "Spring Cleaning", "Studebakers as Circus Stars", "A Summer Day, 1937", "Things We Loved Too Much", "A *True* Story", "The Unexpected Gift", "Vittles, Vehicles American Style", "A Vintage Accessory We'll Never See Again", "Where Did You Go? Out. What Did You Do? Nothing.", "Where We Camped, 1937", "Why Cars Had Runningboards", "A Winter's Tale", "Zern's Zany Nash".

"Downhill Racers" appeared in *Goodguys Gazette*.

© 2011 Albert Drake
Design and Production by Monica Drake-Alonso, Linda Candello-Drake and Moss Drake. Squirrel Knob photos by Paul W. Long.

Throttle Press
P.O. Box 66874
Portland, OR 97290-6874

ISBN 0-936892-20-X
Printed in U.S.A.

Table of Contents

Overtures to Motion

Introduction

I was born right smack in the middle of the Great Depression, and grew up during World War II.

Those were tough times, and yet, had I been able to choose, I could not have chosen to have been born during a better time period. Charles Dickens could have been writing about the 1930s and 1940s instead of the French Revolution when he wrote: "It was the best of times, and it was the worst of times." The Depression, which began in 1929 and lasted through the decade, affected almost everyone. Unemployment was around 25%, which meant that an army of men was competing for every job, including the New Deal Works Progress Administration (WPA) jobs.

World War II was global. It ripped young men from school and work, away from ordinary, civilized life, and sent them to distant places, where they were required to kill or be killed. Many did, and many were. During the first decade of my life there was economic chaos followed by a war in which millions died. That was the worst of times.

In that light, it's difficult to say how anything about that time period could make it the "best", but so much happened that changed our lives, often for the better, and those things have to be acknowledged. Also, I speak from the personal perspective of a boy living in America, sheltered from much of the "worst."

I've read that one's personality is formed during the first six months, or the first five years, depending on which authority you consult. In either case, a kid is helpless to control his environment or heredity. What I heard during those early years, especially from my mother, was that we were "broke." Then for the next five years the ominous clouds of war hung in the sky. That was how the Depression and the war affected me at the time, and, to a degree, still do years later.

I loved comic books, and had a box of them that I read until the pages were ragged. But I hardly ever bought a comic book; a dime was a considerable sum. Mainly I got them from friends who would throw them away after one reading. I read them repeatedly and saved them, in part because I didn't have a dime to buy another. I came to appreciate some more than others, and occasionally I'd take the latter to a used book store near my house where I traded them, two for one.

That was a microcosm of the times: it was possible to find pleasure for little or no money.

It's also a timely example; comic books that reprinted newspaper funny strips became popular in the 1930s, and the first original comic book appeared in 1938, just as I was beginning to read. Had they emerged years later I might not have been interested in them. I grew up with Superman, Captain Marvel, Batman and Robin and others, even as they were growing up.

Every day I looked forward to reading the newspaper, primarily for the funnies. In those days, unlike today, most strips were built around a continuous narrative, and I *had* to read "Dick Tracy", "Terry and the Pirates", "Smilin' Jack", "Little Orphan Annie", "Wash Tubbs", et al. to see what dire situation was unfolding. A strip like "Li'l Abner" might have two, perhaps three plots going at once; the strip was funny, bizarre, well-crafted, with dialogue and events such as Sadie Hawkins Day and the Shmoo that have become part of our popular culture.

Every day, after reading the funnies, I'd flip through the paper to the radio program listing and draw a circle around the programs I intended to listen to that afternoon and evening. I didn't want to miss anything good, but I couldn't listen to all of them. On a weekday after school I'd catch "Terry and the Pirates" at 5:00, and then move the needle on the dial of the radio in the front room to "Superman" at 5:15. But wait! "Dick Tracy" was on another station at the same time, and I'd be faced with a dilemma. Same problem, different shows, when "Tom Mix" and "Jack Armstrong" were both on at 5:30.

And so on into the night, when I'd listen to programs like "Henry Aldrich", "The Old Ranger", "The Lone Ranger", "Death Valley Days", "Red Ryder", "It Pays to be Ignorant", and a very scary "Inner Sanctum". Saturday night I would not miss "Gang Busters", with its vivid sound effects. Although programs shifted time slots, often on a Sunday I could listen to Gene Autry's "Melody Ranch" and "The Shadow" in the afternoon and "The Jack Benny Show" and "Sam Spade" at night.

I loved those programs, and many others. Sometimes we're able to visit the past, and are disappointed. A house where we once lived is smaller than remembered, a particular car is not as much fun to drive, a certain old movie disappoints. In recent years I've listened to many of my favorite radio programs from the 1940s on tape, and they have lost none of their appeal. I still like to go to bed, turn out the lights and play, for example, a 1944 program featuring "The Whistler"—in a minute the darkness around me becomes 1944! The story is compelling, and the production qualities—sound effects, organ music, narrator's voice—are excellent. It's especially remarkable when we realize that the people working on a particular program might be responsible for two other programs broadcast that same day.

The same is true for old comic books I've been able to re-read. Many still hold my attention, and some sweep me back to a time when I was a kid, lying in a hammock in the back yard, on a hot day, the air lazy with the thick odor of cedar. When I read a copy of "Daredevil", "Boy", or "Crime Does Not Pay", I enter the world of my youth.

My view of the war was filtered through those comic books, where superheroes fought the Axis on all fronts. These included the members of the Justice Society of America—Green Lantern, Flash, Atom, Dr. Fate,

Hawkman, Hourman and Sandman—which was formed as the war began and disappeared soon after it ended.

Of course the war loomed large in the movies made during the 1940s. The enemy was everywhere, with Nazi and Fascist forces in Europe, and the Japanese in the Pacific; at home the most normal-looking people turned out to be spies. Most of those movies have probably turned to dust, but I'd love to see, say, "Corvette K-225", a film I told my chums about until they'd had enough, or "China's Little Devils", about Chinese kids helping a handful of American soldiers fight the Japanese.

The other popular film genre was the western, and sometimes the land grabbers and bank robbers that Gene Autry and Roy Rogers fought turned out to be working for the Axis powers. Whatever variation of the western was presented, we were enraptured—we couldn't get enough! I'm not being critical; perhaps we knew those westerns and war films were shot in a Hollywood studio or in the Mojave Desert. It didn't matter. We entered into the verisimilitude of the screen image, and believed that whatever we were shown was "real."

I went to the Saturday matinee as often as possible, usually at the Aero Theater, only a few blocks from my house. A ticket for a kid was about twenty cents, and less, I think, for the matinee. For that I got to see a cartoon, an adventure serial, the newsreel and one, sometimes two, feature films. Hours later I'd ride my bike home and it'd be a horse, a race car, a plane, a space ship—whatever the movie had been about.

I lived at the edge of the city, and less than a mile away was Indian Rock, an abandoned stone quarry, whose topography resembled that of many western films. Sometimes I'd ride my bike there, tearing up and down the trails, reenacting some scene from a movie. Not far from its base was Johnson Creek, and often, in the summer, I'd find a raft and pole it around the deeper parts like Tom Sawyer. Or I'd climb Mt. Scott, a hike that could last all day. I'd ride my bike around the neighborhood, picking berries or apples, whatever was in season, to eat or throw. Sometimes I'd ride to the drug store in Lents and read comic books until the pharmacist kicked me out.

Most of the things I did were free, or, like the movies, cost little. I spent hours at the local library, reading a wide range of books on cars, chemistry, hunting and fishing. I'd walk through the vacant fields in my neighborhood, carrying my Daisy Red Ryder model B-B gun, playing out scenes from war movies. If I had a few cents to spend I might join in a trend, such as playing marbles in the spring on the playground before school, or getting a Duncan yo-yo, or a plastic pea shooter and a bag of dried peas. There was always something to do and I was never bored.

All this came together when I turned 15 and became seriously interested in cars. I read about them in the new magazines, *Road and Track*, *Hot Rod* and *Motor Trend*; as with the superheroes, I was growing up with the car magazines as they were growing up. Had I been born earlier, there would have been little or nothing to read about either cars or comics. The new magazines also meant that there was increased interest in hopping up engines and modifying cars. Suddenly, all over America boys and young men were taking old cars and making them lower, faster and better than new. And they were taking new cars and making them lower, faster, and, I thought, better.

I knew nothing about cars, so everything was new to me. If I saw a Model A parked somewhere that appeared to be a little different—perhaps it had 16" wheels—I had to squat to see whether it had hydraulic brakes, then peer through the hood louvers to see if it had a downdraft carburetor, or possibly two! If I saw a new 1950 Ford with duals, I'd spend a few minutes just looking at the twin chrome extensions.

If I saw a car that had more work than that done to it, I'd go crazy. In 1950 most cars on the road were older, and because no new cars had been built during WW II there was an abundance of cars from the 1930s and even the 1920s still on the road. They were tall and had dull paint, and if I saw a stripped roadster or coupe, something that stood out from the other cars, I'd pursue it on my bike, hoping to catch it at the next stop light. On one occasion I was riding the city bus, en route to my job as a theater usher, when I saw a neat 1936 Ford 3-window coupe parked at a small restaurant. I got off the bus to check the coupe out. I didn't have another nickel for the fare to get back on the bus, but it didn't seem to matter. I had to walk the rest of the way to work.

I was interested in almost every car I saw, especially those old gray cars from decades past, because I knew that that was where any car I might get would come from. I knew I had been born at the right time, because in 1950, when I was 15, there were so many old cars to choose from. They were parked in yards or in garages, or were still being driven. The used car lots along 82nd Avenue, a main street near my house, were loaded with possible buys. One lot had a large sign that said, "No Car Over $99"! I wish I had a photo of that lot, because I'm certain that at one time or another it had every kind of car, from Austin to Zephyr, and I suspect it might have had an occasional Cord or classic Cadillac.

I didn't have $99, but I was trying to save for a car. I clearly remember a conversation between two guys I went to high school with, even though today they don't remember me! I was standing beside the road with some other guys after a day of picking beans, and these two guys from school drove out in a Model A coupe. At some point, one said that they were finding Model A Fords "for five or ten dollars." The reason I remember the moment and the conversation so clearly was because I wanted a car and I had *that* kind of money!

The curbs were not lined with parked cars the way they are today—in fact, most streets around my neighborhood did not have curbs—but the older cars were often parked in the driveway, or beside the house or in a back yard; you had to look. There were plenty of vacant lots and open spaces where a car, or its parts, might be found. When I did my paper route I'd find an

4

abandoned chassis or engine, and I'd try to imagine how I could get that stuff home. Near the end of the route was the start of what has today become a huge wrecking yard, but at that time there were junked cars and parts in the weeds. Near the dirt road was an inline engine, a six or eight cylinder flathead—I have no idea what it was, although I somehow thought it was a Packard—and I imagined getting that huge thing home in my wagon! I knew where an old Ford chassis was, and a 1926 Model T coupe body had been discarded in the swampy land east of my house. I imagined how I could get all those parts home, and somehow merge them into a running car.

Everything seemed so simple! Perhaps I got my ideas for assembling a machine from comic books I'd read and movies I'd seen. Or I got them from reading a copy of *Dyke's* or *Page's Motor Manual* at the library. These were books where simplified drawings of a car like a Model T Ford gave the impression that building a real car was essentially like building a model car. Less than 50 years earlier Henry Ford had built his first engine in his kitchen; it seemed entirely possible to combine a bunch of mismatched, cast-off parts in the driveway.

Another reason the idea of building a car seemed so simple to me was because cars were simple. I had seen my father do a valve job at home in a day, and dismantle and reassemble an engine in a weekend. On the earlier cars the hood could be removed quickly, and even into the 1940s the engine was accessible. Unlike the cars of today, those cars were incredibly basic; if an engine had fuel and spark, and was in time, it'd run. I could visualize the internal workings of an engine in my head. Sometimes in dreams the machinery was an extension of my body, where I would be part of a car; cars were that personal, and not at all complex.

Life, too, was simple, which is a reason the 1940s and 1950s are called the good old days. After I turned sixteen I began to buy cars for $25 to $50. Usually I didn't have to register the car in my name, and often I didn't have insurance; sometimes the license plates were expired. I'm not in favor of such behavior today, but in those days, if I could buy a car for, say, $25, it seemed wrong to spend twice that amount to insure the car for a year. I'd buy a car, get the title and drive it, not worrying about the cops. Cops were seldom seen anyway.

Right or wrong, it's that sense of personal freedom that characterized the times. You could park old cars in the yard or on the street without breaking the social contract in the same way that you could burn leaves and yard cuttings at home, without fear that a busybody neighbor lady would call the cops. People left other people alone. That kind of freedom, along with cheap cars, cheap gas and little traffic, are only memories today, but they're worth remembering.

OH! BABY!

erton, 4306 Southeast Harrison, March 30, a
son, Sidney E.
    Drake—To Mr. and Mrs. A. H. Drake,
3704 North Omaha, March 26, a son.
    Evans—To Mr. and Mrs. G. D. Evans, 218

Wheels

First there was the baby buggy, then the stroller. With help, he could leave the house. Without help and those two vehicles, the world was only three rooms, where he crawled from the sofa to the old claw-foot dining room table. Sun came through the organdy curtains and lay in a block on the wooden floor, evoking odors of varnish and wax. Beside the square of sun-warmed floor was a sheet of newspaper. His mother was ironing, and as she ironed she sang: "Oh give me a nail and a hammer, and a picture to hang on the wall." It was pleasant, with the sun and the song. The air smelled of hot fabric. In the paper was an ad with a pair of lower case g's; they looked like two coffee percolators. Then his mother folded a dress and sang: "A sweet little nest, 'way out in the West."

When he woke his mother was dressing him to go out. She wore a patterned long dress. He wore a cap and jacket. On the sidewalk the sun was warm, the air cool. The ridges on the concrete squares sent vibrations up his back. He wanted to go on, but his mother turned around, toward the house. In the shadow now it was cooler. His mother was not singing. There was no movement on the sidewalk or on the street, and it was as if there were only two people in the world.

There were three people in the world when his father took them on a Sunday drive. The floor vibrated, then smoothed, then vibrated as the car picked up speed. Buildings moved past, and sometimes a truck. The air in the car was blue, with an odor like sweet milk. As the car went faster the vibrations got stronger, and he was lulled into sleep.

He woke at the edge of a golf course. There was a long line of tall poplar trees, moving in the breeze. There was the green smell of cut grass. As his mother and father talked the sun went down and it got dark.

The Unexpected Gift

In an essayish short story, John Updike wrote: "the unexpected gift is worth giving." That line pops into my head each Christmas as I search the stores for things that loved ones will want to receive. We all want to please, to look a little harder for the special gift, and often it isn't a matter money but of thought. Our reward for our efforts is the look of anticipation, then pleasure, when the recipient unwraps the gift, and then we know we did exactly the right thing.

But if a lack of money is an obstacle it's harder to please anyone, regardless of one's intentions. My father loved to celebrate Christmas, but I know there were times, especially when he and my mother were newly-married, when money was a real problem. That was in the middle of the Depression when, as my mother often mentioned, they did not have salt for the beans. That first Christmas in Portland they lived in a tent; my father was out looking for work, and as he walked the streets he picked up old cigarette packages, took them home and cut up the tinfoil inner wrapper to use as tinsel on the tree he had got somewhere.

In this context, and faced with the question of how to get me a Christmas present, he simply took two of my toy cars, sanded them smooth and painted them new colors. I was apparently greatly pleased with what I thought were new cars, and it was years before I learned what he had done. At the time I was happy, my father was happy, and the simple act of recycling those toy cars seemed to embody the true meaning of Christmas.

Only in looking back can I discern—or create—a bit of pathos. I imagine my father applying the new paint, just as he sometimes painted his full-size car with a brush and a can of enamel, and I wonder whether he felt anger, regret, guilt at not being able to buy his only child a new toy?

If so, he figured out a way to compensate. He put each car in a box, wrapped it with a page from the Sunday comics, then put that within another box and wrapped it. From stores he got other boxes of various sizes, and he fitted one within another until the final box was large enough to hold a tricycle. I can remember opening box after box, only to find another box within, and my parents laughing at my perplexed expression as this charade went on and on, like something from a Marx Brothers' movie. The boxes got smaller and smaller until, to my infinite pleasure, within the final box I found the strange toy car, smelling of new paint, the center of all that wrapping and unwrapping like the heart of an artichoke.

A Nearly-Modern Story Book

The Modern Story Book, a book for children, was first published in 1931; what defines its modernity is its emphasis on the machines developed during the first three decades of the century. Instead of a children's story about a king in a far-off land, there is the story of an airplane that attempts to fly to the sun (which, of course, is a retelling of the Greek myth of Icarus). Instead of the runaway gingerbread man there is the story of the runaway elevator. But these were hard-edged fairy tales for many youthful readers who, in 1931, had never seen an elevator or an airplane, and barely understood them as concepts.

I got the book years after 1931, when I was five and beginning to read books aimed at older readers; this was my first experience with anthropomorphism—the attribution of human characteristics to inanimate objects—and a couple of the stories struck me as being pretty strange. The main characters in the stories are machines that take on human qualities, and therefore they are heroic, foolish, stubborn, angry, joyful, tired, ill, or grow old.

A steam shovel loses her appetite, and balks at eating more dirt. A dirigible, caught in a severe storm, stubbornly ignores the commander's orders, which he knows are wrong, and gets back to the hangar safely. A switch engine becomes depressed when he learns he will never become a full-sized engine, but when he's needed he pulls a passenger train and finds happiness. A wall fan, named Fanny Blowhard, suffers ridicule by other things in the room, who do not consider her a respectable piece of office equipment, and so she blows until there is chaos.

A story that has remained in my mind for years concerns a machine that shows heroic qualities. An old fire truck, "one of the first automobile fire engines ever made," and his old driver find little to do until a skyscraper catches fire. Then they pump water from a dangerous position behind the building, and because the story takes place in mid-winter, the engine is soon covered with ice. That's the image that I always remember: The little engine hidden under the ice, with an eye drawn on the only headlight that is showing. The wall falls, but the fireman crawls under the engine and is saved. After the event the fire engine and the fireman are rescued, repaired, and celebrated as heroes.

In fact, all the machines in these stories triumph, redeem themselves, or accommodate themselves to their situation—all except one. "The Lazy Automobile" is the story of Chuffer, a touring car that has grown old and lazy when the story opens. One Sunday the car's owner, Mr. Smiggles, loads the car up with eight people for a pleasure drive. Chuffer feels resentful, and perhaps because of the weight of his passengers, he falls asleep in busy city traffic. Later he falls asleep in the middle of a huge mud puddle, and everyone has to wade through the mud and somehow get home. Mr. Smiggles stays with the car.

When a mechanic, who can't get the car to start, offers five dollars for Chuffer, Mr. Smiggles takes it. Still asleep, Chuffer is towed "to a big open lot where hundreds and hundreds of automobiles stood." He wakes the next morning, and asks the car beside him what's going on. "This is an automobile graveyard. When an automobile gets so lazy that he won't run any more, they bring him here and take out all his parts which are worth anything. Then they leave the rest of him to rust away."

Chuffer is repentant, but it's too late. The author's voice tells us that Chuffer fell asleep, "And he is probably sleeping yet. For what had happened to him is just what usually happens to automobiles when they become so old and lazy that they will not run anymore."

In the story was a moral for children who understood that laziness should be avoided. In a literal way, they also learned that as cars got older they became undependable. The subtext of the story was that new cars are good: a message that we still hear in advertising. But in 1931, when this book was published, the new car dealers were encouraged to smash the head and block on older cars, and to amass huge piles of old cars and set the piles afire as a way of creating a market for new cars.

Death and rebirth is the stuff of myth, and it's interesting that in a later version of the book, Chuffer didn't die. A reader, Stan How, sent word that in his 1942 edition Chuffer has an opportunity to redeem himself and he starts on "the first whirr (sic) of the starter." The garage man calls Mr. Smiggles, who comes and gets the car. Chuffer "ran so beautifully all the way home that Mr. Smiggles decided he wouldn't trade him even for a brand new car." This change in the story was no doubt the result of the wartime automobile shortage. Chuffer's change of attitude was complete—at least for the duration!

THE GARAGE MAN AND HIS HELPER BEGAN TO TAKE OUT CHUFFER'S ENGINE

Machines

My father grew up in a small town, Westhope, North Dakota, one of nine children. My mother grew up on a nearby farm in Landa, one of nine children. Perhaps they met when he drove a tractor or threshing machine on her father's farm at harvest time, for she helped cook for the threshing crew. Or perhaps she came to Westhope to see a moving picture show, and saw my father zooming along the main street in his stripped-down Model T.

I heard the stories, how he got an old car running and drove it when he was twelve. Every farm had a windbreak of trees and the farmer parked his equipment there, the water wagon, grain wagon and stonebolt, along with the cars and trucks that had quit running. Besides the Fords and Chevrolets, the extended grove might hold Dorts, Wintons, Chalmers and a hundred other short-lived makes, all available for a kid who had mechanical ideas.

I heard how my father built a snow buggy from parts, a story told so many times it became part of the family mythology. He got a chassis, put skis at all four corners, mounted the engine in the rear and built a drive off the flywheel. The engine turned a propeller, which pushed the machine over snowy fields at a good clip. He ordered the propeller from a magazine ad, and it cost a huge sum, $14.00, I believe. When it broke, he whittled another prop from a chunk of wood, and he bragged that it worked as well as the one he'd bought.

That was pretty much how things went all his life. If he wanted something he had to make it himself, or improvise the best he could. He was a good carpenter, and able to do his own electrical wiring and plumbing. He could fabricate and adapt and switch parts and juryrig; not everything lasted, but he had to try.

My parents married and came to Oregon in 1934, in the middle of a severe economic Depression. There were no jobs, but he somehow found work in service stations where he pumped gas, did oil changes and greased cars, did brake jobs and tune ups. Machines were so simple in those days he no doubt did engine overhauls too, without benefit of a micrometer. He could approximate a valve job using a suction stick and lapping compound, and did not need to worry about taper or piston clearances.

In the same natural way, my father seemed able to drive any vehicle, from a motorcycle to a bulldozer. He graduated to WPA jobs, working in the woods and on Bonneville dam, wherever a piece of equipment needed to be driven or worked on. During WW II he worked in both Swan Island and Oregon Shipyards, where he drove a whirley crane. He had to climb a ladder to the cab, which was 100 feet in the air. I wondered how could he do that?—meaning, how could he know how to operate that huge crane and also how could he climb that ladder every day?

Al Drake "skinning cat" in the Tillamook Burn in 1938. He came from North Dakota, a state as flat as a board, where every turn is a right angle, so he must have been thrilled when got to Oregon, with all its topography. This was a W.P.A. (Works Progress Administration) job, an agency set up by President Roosevelt to create work for an army of unemployed men during the Depression. This was useful work, creating the highway from Portland to the coast. It went through the coastal mountains in an area that had suffered three major forest fires during the 1930s, which is why there's no standing timber. Note that this cat uses cables, not a hydraulic system, to raise and lower the blade.

A Summer Day, 1937

There are several things of interest in this photo of my father and me taken in 1937. I'm sure of the year, because I know where we lived then, but I questioned the time of the year, trying to determine exactly how old I was and whether my feet could reach the pedals of my first car. Judging by my thin clothing, it's obviously summer, and the shadows suggest it's around noon on a sunny day. The rose bushes are in full bloom, dandelions have already gone to seed and the lawn desperately needs mowing.

I'm struck by the lack of distractions in the photo. There are no people around, and the only car parked on the street is blocks away. It matches the mental photo of the 1930s that I carry around, but I'm always surprised to see those open streets. It was a typical suburban neighborhood, but I guess even on this sunny day the neighbors all kept their cars in the garage or at least well back from the street.

Another thing that interests me is the stack of wood piled between the street and the sidewalk two houses away. I know now that it was called "slab wood," the outer rounded pieces of a tree that were removed so that the tree could be cut into lumber. Today we consider that a waste of good wood, which it was. But that was the practice 70 years ago, and I suspect the slabs sold during the Depression for very little, even after they were delivered and stacked.

Before the fall rains began a man would come through the neighborhood with an old flatbed truck, or occasionally an old car made into a flatbed truck. He had an engine mounted on the bed, a Ford Model T or A or some other four-cylinder engine, and in place of the flywheel he had mounted a circular saw blade perhaps three feet in diameter. The blade hung over the edge of the flatbed, and was completely unguarded.

When he fired up that engine that huge blade spun rapidly, gleaming in the sun. He'd run a slab of wood through the blade, cutting the slab into a half-dozen furnace-sized pieces, and the neighborhood would echo with each shriek of the blade. He'd throw the cut pieces on the ground, and someone, usually an older boy, would carry them to a basement window and throw them through the opening where they'd be burned in the furnace during the winter.

This same process was going on a dozen years later at the grade school I attended. Today it's impossible to imagine anyone sawing wood in a suburban neighborhood with that flashing, shrieking naked blade cutting the air!

The focus of the photograph is the pedal car, which, I think, I got that day. Even more remarkable than that naked, screaming saw blade is the fact that I got a new car! Most of my toys were quite used, often repainted by my father, but since they were new to me I was happy with them. This pedal car appears to be new, and modeled after a 1935 Ford grille—the headlights and other details, anyway—although those side panels recall a 1936 Plymouth.

Years later, thanks to Al Stewart, I learned that the car was a 1936 La Salle, Number 1613. At the time, I didn't know the make, but the pedal car had lots of neat things, like headlights and taillights, an imitation gear shift lever, a bulb horn and that fold-down windshield. I must have been happy. Who would not be, even in the middle of a Depression?

The Sidewalk Flyer: An Appreciation

In the beginning there was the wheel, and little more. This is where we all began, whether we had a sidewalk flyer or simply saw someone riding one—someone fortunate enough to live in a neighborhood with sidewalks. It represented unearned motion, the joys of gravity. All one needed was a little push, a slight slope, and seemingly without effort the wind tugged at your hair and the world rushed past. It was the closest a kid could come to flying, at least until he got a bicycle.

The parts could be found in almost any basement or back alley. Take one old sidewalk skate, cut it in two and nail the halves to the bottom of a 2x4. Nail an upright wooden soap box to the base, and a pair of handles on top to steer it by. Everything else is decoration: paint, twin tuna fish cans for headlights, an automobile hood ornament, and a defunct license plate.

This means of locomotion was a product of the Depression, when you had to make your own fun, and it wound down in popularity when soapboxes were made of cardboard. Then kids got real scooters, then bicycles. Today's version is the skateboard. If sidewalk flyer owners hoped to someday own a Model A Ford, to what do skateboarders aspire?

Where We Camped, 1937

At the top of the photo my mother wrote the necessary words to remind me of that time almost beyond my memory: "Where we camped two days in July `37." Because I've looked at the photo occasionally it's become familiar—more familiar than the event itself—and I have to calculate on my fingers to realize that it was over 70 years ago that my parents and I stayed in the cabin pictured in the photo.

How the world has changed in three score plus years. America was in economic chaos, World War II was a few years off, and before it ended the world would enter the Atomic Age. The decades tumble through my mind, like the pages of a calendar in a movie, time blowing away on a metaphorical

wind. The optimism of the later 1940s, the energetic 1950s, the tumultuous 1960s, then the 1970s, 1980s, 1990s, decades that went past so quickly it's hard to describe them.

Suddenly it's the 21st century, and everything has changed so drastically that that 1937 campground represents the distant past. It could be the Alamo, or the setting for the Battle of Hastings.

In 1937 the Depression was in full swing. That was the year that the Joad family migrated from Oklahoma to California in John Steinbeck's novel *The Grapes of Wrath*, and although fictional characters, they represented the thousands of people who actually made the journey. To realize how poor people could be in the 1930s, take a look at *Let Us Now Praise Famous Men*, the book that resulted from James Agee and Walker Evan's stay with three white sharecropper families in the South.

We were poor, the people we knew were poor, and I assumed everyone was pretty poor. Because we didn't have a refrigerator we used condensed milk which my mother thinned with water. She washed clothes on the back porch in a wooden machine with an electric motor. She cooked on a wood stove summer and winter, which meant that someone had to get up early to start that fire. She darned socks and sewed patches on patches by hand. My father worked at laboring jobs, where a shovel was a well-known tool, or in service stations and garages.

We did own a radio, which I loved, and a car, a 1932 Ford tudor, which was no doubt what got us to this campground for two days. The concept of a vacation seemed strange. My parents had to work to keep going day by day, and to take a vacation meant going some place, which we rarely did. Even into the 1950s my father's idea of a vacation was to load up the family car, and drive up an old logging road in the coastal mountains. When the road ended we'd pitch a large tent and stay two or three days. Except for a trip to San Francisco and two trips to North Dakota, one because of a family emergency, we rarely went anywhere, and a vacation seemed like an excuse to get away from home.

So in 1937 the campground must've looked like heaven. It's on a postcard, and the writing at the bottom notes that this is "On the grounds of the Nelscott Auto Court," located on the Oregon coast. The first building is

At Mt. Hood Lodge. (July '38)

This photo might have been taken on the day that Timberline Lodge, located on Mt. Hood, was dedicated. My father is hanging on to me, while my mother, who stands beside him, looks apprehensive. The long wheelbase sightseeing vehicle is probably based on the new Chrysler. The woman to the left is fashionably dressed with a belted jacket, culottes, sombrero and sunglasses. Such glasses were rare before the war, as were pants on women.

the office, and it looks better than the house my parents were then renting. Behind it is the Community Kitchen, where families cooked and ate their meals. To the left there's a building that might be the showers, with perhaps even a washing machine.

I can imagine my mother getting excited about the prospect of hot water; on the farm where she grew up the water had to be heated on the wood stove and the family members bathed, one by one, in a tub in the kitchen near the stove. At the Nelscott Auto Camp there was a gas stove on which my mother could cook pancakes and fried eggs, perhaps bacon or ham, and make coffee.

Then we walked to the beach, where I dug in the sand with a tin shovel. I hated the gritty sand that collected under my wool bathing suit. My father would take off his shirt, and he'd stand for hours puffing on his pipe or a hand rolled cigarette, staring at the constant waves, a sight which could be compared to acres of grain waving the wind but which was really as far from anything he might have seen in North Dakota as one could imagine. That was what a vacation meant to him, while for my mother it was cooking a meal over a gas flame. For me it was the experience of getting sand everywhere and then getting into the shower, shedding my itchy wool bathing suit and feeling the warm water wash away the grit. No one can measure another's sense of pleasure. Those were our pleasures, and they were as real as anything one might experience on the French Riviera or, later, at Disneyland.

KGW at 10:30 P. M. The story titled "Skyway to the East," tells of the need for amicable relations between the United States and Russia before the skyway can become a reality. Tommy Dorsey will combine

Adele Anderson, dramatic soprano, who will sing song cycles in recitals on three successive Mondays at Portland School of Music, commencing Monday.

...ers are those of the other opera companies, and the San Francisco Opera orchestra is generally conceded to be best of its kind in the country. Its members are also members of the San Francisco symphony which keeps them together for a longer period of time each year than the members of other opera orchestras.

Members of the San Francisco ballet directed by Willam Christensen are also part of the Opera personnel.

The casts for the four operas to be produced here include leading San Francisco and Metropolitan stars — American and European—with outstanding supporting artists. Libero Djanel and Raoul Jobin will sing the roles of Carmen and Don Jose in Bizet's opera. Licia Albanese and Charles Kullman will be Violetta and Alfredo in Verdi's "La Traviata." Set Svanholm, Swedish dramatic tenor, will make his North American debut in the title role of Wagner's "Lohengrin" with Astrid Varnay as Elsa. Dorothy Kirsten will sing Mimi in the Puccini opera "La Boheme." Charles Kullman will sing the part of Rodolfo, and Ezio Pinza will be heard as Colline. Salvatore Baccaloni, who sang here with his Commedia dell' Arte players last March, will also...

Radio Programs—Sunday, Aug. 4

	KGW NBC Net 620 kc.	KEX ABC Net 1190 kc.	KOIN CBS Net 970 kc.	KALE MBS Net 1330 kc.
6:00	Bible Highlights		Church of the Air	
6:15	Bible Highlights		Church of the Air	
6:30	Voices Down Wind		Church of the Air	
6:45	Voices Down Wind		Church of the Air	
7:00	The Eternal Light	Message. of Israel	W. Sweeney, News	Radio Bible Class
7:15	The Eternal Light	Message. of Israel	Wings Over Jordan	Radio Bible Class
7:30	News Highlights	Southernaires	Salt L. Tabernacle	1g. Peoples Church
7:45	Paul Page Sings	Southernaires	Salt L. Tabernacle	1g. Peoples Church
8:00	Church in Home*	Builders of Faith	Inv. to Learning	Pilgrim Hour
8:15	Church in Home*	Dr. Ralph Walker	Inv. to Learning	Pilgrim Hour
8:30	Concert Orch.	Strictly Music*	Sincerely Yours	Lutheran Hour
8:45	Concert Orch.	Strictly Music*	Sincerely Yours	Lutheran Hour
9:00	America United	Strictly Music*	People's Platform	News*
9:15	America United	Strictly Music*	People's Platform	The Funnies*
9:30	Round Table	Sunday Strings	Time for Reason	Choir*
9:45	Round Table	Sunday Strings	News*	Choir*
10:00	American Music	Cliff Edwards	Assignment Home	Glen Hardy
10:15	American Music	Orson Welles	Assignment Home	Commander Scott
10:30	Harvest of Stars	Sammy Kaye Ser,	News Review	Old Songs*
10:45	Harvest of Stars	Sammy Kaye Ser.	News Review	Sunday Favorite
11:00	Carmen Cavallaro	Sam Balter	Columbia Symphon	Band Concert
11:15	Carmen Cavallaro	Music for Sunday	Columbia Symphon	Band Concert
11:30	One Man's Family	Music for Sunday	Columbia Symphon	Bill Cunningham
11:45	One Man's Family	America's Future	Columbia Symphon	Veterans Program
12:00	The National Hour	Elmer Davis	Columbia Workshop	News*
12:15	The National Hour	The Vagabonds	Columbia Workshop	This Chase
12:30	XavierCugatOrch.	Down Your Alley	Summer Hour	Detective Play
12:45	News*	Down Your Alley	Summer Hour	Detective Play
1:00	Symphony Orch.	Darts for Dough	Family Hour	Music*
1:15	Symphony Orch.	Darts for Dough	Family Hour	Christian Science*
1:30	Symphony Orch.	Counterspy	Front Porch	Abbott Mystery
1:45	Symphony Orch.	Counterspy	William Shirer	Abbott Mystery
2:00	The Catholic Hour	Sunday Party	Silver Theater	Those Websters
2:15	The Catholic Hour	Sunday Party	Silver Theater	Those Websters
2:30	Oregon Album*	Eugenie Baird	Hope Chest	Sunday at Home*
2:45	Oregon Album*	Eugenie Baird	Hope Chest	Sweetheart Time
3:00	Frank Morgan	Drew Pearson	Gene Autry	Let's Go to Opera
3:15	Frank Morgan	Don Gardner	Gene Autry	Let's Go to Opera
3:30	Rogue's Gallery	Hollyw'dSmashhit!	What I Would Say	CBC Star Show
3:45	Rogue's Gallery	Hollyw'dMusicHall	News*	CBC Star Show
4:00	Alec Templeton	Music Festival	Richard Lawless	Auto Races*
4:15	Alec Templeton	Music Festival	Richard Lawless	Auto Races*
4:30	Tommy Dorsey	Music Festival	Money on the Line	Open House
4:45	Tommy Dorsey	Music Festival	Money on the Line	Open House
5:00	Merry-Go-Round	News	Curtiss Archer	Romantic Cycle*
5:15	Merry-Go-Round	Lorella Parsons	Curtiss Archer	Romantic Cycle*
5:30	Familiar Music	Jimmie Fidler	Star Theater	Spl. Investigator
5:45	Familiar Music	Police Woman	Star Theater	News
6:00	Hour of Charm	Hour of Mystery	Take It or Leave It	Exploring Unknown
6:15	Hour of Charm	Hour of Mystery	Take It or Leave It	Exploring Unknown
6:30	Rhythm Rhapsody	Hour of Mystery	F. Mills & Strings	Double or Nothing
6:45	Rhythm Rhapsody	Hour of Mystery	F. Mills & Strings	Double or Nothing
7:00	Ask Me Another	Studio	Crime Doctor	Mystery My Hobby
7:15	Ask Me Another	Cavenaugh Trio	Crime Doctor	Mystery My Hobby
7:30	Symphony Hour	Stump the Authors	Blondie	Name That Song
7:45	Symphony Hour	Stump the Authors	Blondie	Name That Song
8:00	Symphony Hour	Network	Crooks Cruise	Hinson Church
8:15	Symphony Hour	Network	Treasury Salute*	Hinson Church
8:30	Frank Morgan	Quiz Kids	Defense Rests	Winchell Program
8:45	Frank Morgan	Quiz Kids	Defense Rests	Sheilah Graham
9:00	Jerry Wald Orch.	Report to People	Man Named Jordan	Glen Hardy
9:15	Jerry Wald Orch.	Report to People	Man Named Jordan	Rex Miller
9:30	G. Benedict Orch.	Songs Good Cheer*	Favorite Playhouse	Singing Sentinels
9:45	Benedies, Organ	This is the Duty	Favorite Playhouse	Ink Spots*
10:00	News Flashes	McCall News*	News*	Romance Passport
10:15	Mary Ann Mercer	Dance Band	University Explores	Romance Passport
10:30	Pacific Story	Sunday Vespers	Vets Bulletin	Inside the News*
10:45	Pacific Story	Sunday Vespers	T. Steele Orch.	Sweet Swing*
11:00	News*	Vera Massey	Dance Orch.	Stan Kenton Orch.
11:15	Music in the Night	Bridge to Dreaml'd	Dance Orch.	Stan Kenton Orch.
11:30	Fitzpatrick Orch.	Bridge to Dreaml'd	Serenade*	Chez Stewart Orch.
11:45	Fitzpatrick Orch.	Bridge to Dreaml'd	Organ	News
12:00	Sign Off		The X-tra Hour	

*Denotes local program.

KWJJ—1080 Kc.
6:15—News
7:00—American Music
12:30—News
12:45—Organist
2:00—Concert Hall
6:15—Waltz Time
6:30—Spotlight

7:00—Sage Riders
8:15—Hawthorne Temple
9:15—News

KXL—750 Kc.
9:05—Scandinavian Hour
10:05—Waltz Time
10:30—Bing Crosby

12:00—News
12:15—Book Chats
12:30—Frank Sinatra
2:15—Baseball
News on the Hour

KGW—FM—95.2 Meg.
3 to 10:50 P. M.

Studebakers as Circus Stars

During the 1930s and early 1940s Clyde Beatty's name was as well known to the public as any movie star or athlete; he was in a sense both those things and more. He made well-publicized trips to Africa where he captured scores of lions, tigers, and other wild animals then brought them back alive. He used them as performers in his business, the Coles Brothers-Clyde Beatty Show, a traveling circus.

During the Depression people were eager for an affordable entertainment, and they flocked to Beatty's circus to see him work his wild animals, armed only with a whip and a chair. He was also the subject of short and feature-length films, so those who missed his shows saw him on the screen. His competitor was Frank "Bring 'em Back Alive" Buck, but *Time* magazine called Beatty the "most celebrated trainer of lions and tigers in the world."

His name and reputation made him an obvious candidate for commercials. In 1937 Studebaker gave Beatty several of its new models to use in his circus, which gave the car immediate exposure. In one stunt Beatty got a full-grown lion and tiger—natural enemies—to pose together on the roof of a new Studebaker.

In another a medium-size dog was trained to gently close the door of the Studebaker with one paw. A magazine ad showing this trick claimed that the "world's first non-slam automobile doors—click lightly, tightly and silently on revolutionary an exclusive rattle-proof rotary latches. Only 1937 Studebakers offer this safety and convenience."

When the show opened at the Hippodrome in New York in March, 1937, the audience was amazed to see a steady stream of clowns exit a new Studebaker. One after another they emerged and stood beside the car, until

there were 15 full-size adults in the group, and these in many cases were rotund people. They had all squeezed into the model advertised as a three passenger car—proof of its "exceptional roominess."

All of these circus stunts were featured in magazine ads. When asked how he spent his free time, Beatty said that he didn't really have any hobbies, "...except to drive my (personal) Studebaker...That's what I call real relaxation!"

Why Cars Had Runningboards

Too young to ride a bicycle even if I had one, I was limited to our small yard. There was no sidewalk, few houses nearby, and beyond were the vacant fields where I could go only with a parent. Within the yard were a million things to engage my attention, and sometimes I would look straight up where a small plane wrote "Pepsi" in cursive on a blue blackboard.

But by late afternoon I tired of all that and longed to see my father. I could not tell time, but some inner clock let me know that he would be along soon. I squatted by the rose bushes in the front yard, and looked toward the corner. A bee worried a clover blossom, its buzz louder than any traffic. A rooster crowed, and the wind carried the odor of the roses. I waited, and finally I heard the sound of an engine, then my father's big, square sedan came around the corner. My heart leaped, and I jumped up and ran toward him.

The meeting had developed into something like a tribal dance. When my father saw me he stopped the car in the road and I ran to greet him. The ground was sharp against my bare feet, the distances great. It was an effort to climb from the road up onto the car's runningboard, and from there I could barely reach the door handle, which I gripped with both hands. My father's work-worn hand reached from the window, pulling me against the door. Then he'd say something like "Ready?" before he put the car in gear and we accelerated home.

In memory both speed and distance have probably become exaggerated. The ride probably lasted for about 20 feet, but as I stood on that wide runningboard, hanging on for dear life, the wind blowing my hair back, the engine's heat coming in waves through the hood louvers, it was as exciting as any carnival ride. Whatever the dangers, I was reassured by my father's hand holding onto me. The running board gave me a place to stand in the world, and that hand held me securely against the dangers of the world as only a father can, and must.

Buddy — June '07

Mid-Depression Packard

The 1939 photograph accompanying this article was taken on vacation. It shows my father, Albert, and three things he loved. First came his family, of course, meaning me (whose hand he's gripping tightly); his wife Hilda (who took the photo); and his daughter Bonnie, who was yet to be born.

His second love was topography, like the Montana mountains that loomed behind us. He was born and grew up in North Dakota, where every turn is not a smooth curve, but a right angle that follows a section line. The land is flat as a board.

He migrated to Oregon, where he skinned cat on steep slopes. The fear of falling is an archetypal fear, embedded in our collective unconscious, but it did not seem to affect him. He probably stopped the car at this point because of the dramatic landscape. I imagine that beyond the Packard the ground drops away, so my mother is standing on this side of the car. *She* had enough fear for several people.

His third love was cars, especially large cars like this 1935 Packard 120, which he bought used. It was a solid four-door flat-back sedan in dusty beige; fast and heavy enough to lap the miles between Oregon and North Dakota in relative comfort.

Space within that flat trunk must have been limited, because I notice that the entire rear seat area is crammed with clothes and bedding. It's a big car, almost as tall as my father. If you asked the man who owned this Packard, he probably would've said it was impressive. He no doubt wanted to impress his folks in North Dakota, like some rich guy in a limousine. And in a way he was rich or richer. Four short years earlier, in 1935, my parents had arrived in Portland, Oregon, by train. For a year, the year that I was born, they lived in a tent pitched in a field high on a bluff overlooking the Willamette River. My father gathered boards, built a floor and half-walls and put the tent over this temporary structure. There was a garbage dump perhaps 50 feet away, and from a crack in the ground a flame burned brightly, the result of methane gas no doubt. My mother cooked meals on that flame. Meanwhile, my father walked the streets in the middle of the Depression looking for work. "Those were lean times," he often said.

My mother was full of contradictions. On the one hand, she was pleased that the Packard represented upward mobility and took us away from that shameful tent. On the other hand, she felt that people should not show off and she accused my father of that because of the car.

The Packard was taking us back to her parents' farm in North Dakota. I don't know what she wanted, and my father probably didn't know either. The funny thing was that, although that long hood suggested a big V-12 or long straight eight was beneath it, the car had, as I recall, a plebeian straight six-cylinder engine.

The 120 was introduced in the 1930s and aimed at those buyers, like my father, who wanted a stately car that suggested wealth, but at an affordable price. This worked. As America began to go back to work in 1937, Packard hit record production of 109,518 cars. Although that six was akin to a Plymouth or Pontiac, this was a fine car to pull us out of a Depression

Bud, Bob, & Jrs. packard.

Clarence Young's *Motor Boys* Had Grit

In the 19th century, Horatio Alger turned from journalism to fiction, and established a reputation as the author of a series of novels for young readers. His main character, a boy, perhaps orphaned, certainly poor, overcomes adversity and eventually triumphs because he has "grit."

This quality is difficult to define; it's a combination of courage, native intelligence, quick-wittedness, honesty, decency, and fortitude. A young man may be poor and come from humble beginnings, but if he has grit he'll overcome adversity and triumph in the end. It was a noble message for young men, and it reflected, we wanted to believe, the qualities of America—a young nation.

The books were hugely popular, and had numerous imitators. One was the Motor Boys series published early in the 1900s and written by Clarence Young. There were nearly two dozen novels in this series, showing the adventures of several teen-age boys and a new invention, the automobile.

To appreciate the books today we have to enter the minds of young people who lived 100 years ago, in a time long before comic books, television or radio, often in places where newspapers were scarce. At the end of a long day of hard work the only pleasure might be an hour spent reading a book. And what of the boy who had heard of an automobile but had never seen one, and who might not see one for another ten years? His longing for the sound of a piston-driven engine must have been intense.

So books like the Motor Boys series filled a need. They allowed boys to travel in their minds over roads that probably did not exist when the series started in 1905.

In the first volume, subtitled "Chums Through Thick and Thin," the Motor Boys, as they called themselves, win "a big, red touring automobile"; it was the grand prize at a motorcycle field meet.

In the second volume, "Overland" (1906), they familiarize themselves with the machine and then set out on a trip that takes them from their home in Cresville, "a village near Boston," all the way to a lost gold mine in Arizona. In the first volume they acquired a nemesis, Noddy Nixon, "a town bully" who committed a robbery and escaped in his father's automobile; Nixon appears in this volume to maintain a level of conflict, and he escapes at the end to show up in later books.

Unlike the characters in the Alger books, two of the boys come from well-to-do homes; Bob Baker's father is "a rich banker" and Ned Slade's father is "a department store proprietor." With the advent of the car, the characters moved up the social ladder so there would be money to finance the expenses of owning a car and making a trip. The elusive quality of grit, still required, can be found in the young boy who naturally has driving skills.

Of interest to us as readers today is the attitude the author and the characters have toward the act of driving. I wonder whether Young had any experience with automobiles, or whether it's the language he uses to describe the mechanics of the car.

Early on the boys get into a race with another touring car; we're never told the makes of the cars, but the Motor Boys have a 40 hp machine and the other is a 90 hp. Many cars in 1906 had engines that developed 35-40 hp, but I've never found one that developed 90 hp. The 1907 Apperson Jack Rabbit was a hot runabout, and it developed an advertised 50-60 hp.

Other terms might be accurate but odd to today's audience. Although the car is going at a fast clip, the author says "low-speed gear came into play," which I think means something different from simply shifting into low. There is also mention of the "speed gears." The driver, called the "steerer," says, "I didn't have the full-speed lever on." I'm aware that cars of that period usually had the gas, choke, and spark levers on the column, but I've never heard of a "full-speed" lever.

These terms were important, because readers hoped to become drivers someday, and these books could instruct them. Although the terminology might be odd, the thrill of the chase was clear. Early on the boys get into a race with a much faster car with an experienced driver. Bob, who happens to be steering, "threw the third-speed clutch into place..." and "advanced the spark [and] turned on more gasolene [sic]...."

Although the odds are against him, Bob feels confident of a victory because "I haven't used the accelerator pedal yet." When he finally does, it gives the car "a momentary burst of speed" and he passes the more powerful car. The driver who lost recognizes that Bob is a "plucky lad"—i.e., he has grit.

Most of the book is given over to the cross-country journey, which must have been an unusual undertaking in 1906. An older man, "an instructor at the Athletic Club," speaks favorably to the boys' parents about the trip.

"Of course, there will be a few troubles, but none that cannot be overcome with a little work. I think the trip is perfectly possible. In fact, you know, autos have gone clear across the continent."

Although their trip takes a good deal of time, the problems are minor. Occasionally a tire "busts" or "collapses." A landslide destroys the car's "dry batteries"; on one occasion the gas tank catches fire, but the problem is easily solved by driving the car into a creek.

The roads are unpaved but fairly smooth. In fact, the novel's sub-text makes an appeal for cross-country travel, and it makes such travel seem easy.

It's not clear where the boys get gasoline at times, but they never run out. Or, maybe that's the element of fantasy in this fiction.

THEY RUSHED TO ONE SIDE, THUNDERING PAST THE AUTO.—*Page* 114.

"TAKE THAT!" NED CRIED.—*Page* 43.

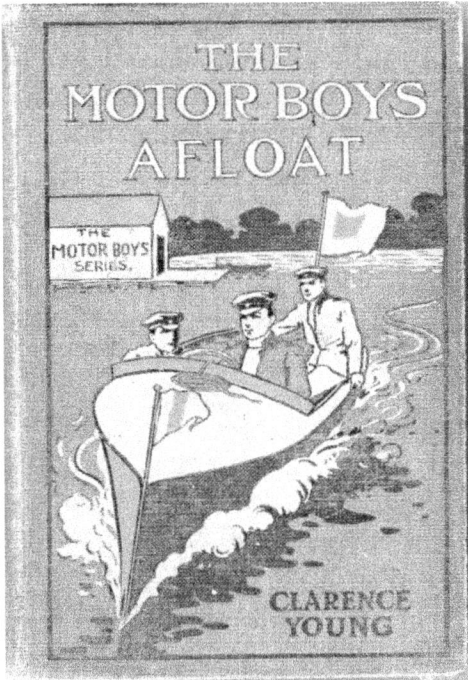

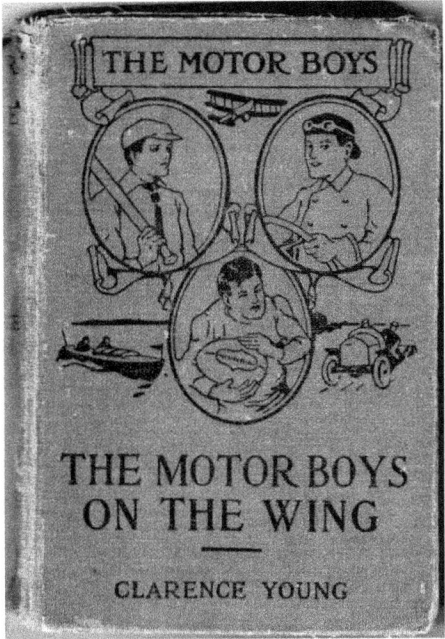

Baked Enamel

Perhaps my father painted only one car, one time, in the driveway. Or, perhaps he painted more than one, because on hot summer days I can still smell the doped odor of enamel that hung heavily in the air when I was a child!

If there was only one then it was some 1933-'34 model, a Nash Lafayette or Oldsmobile, although I can't recall my father owning either of those cars. It was something after cars were square but before they were rounded, something angular, with a sloping grille and pie-shaped or square doors on the hood sides. That I can't recall the car's make does not lessen the intensity of the vision.

Did he prepare the car for paint? I suspect that he did not mask off the glass or minimal chrome. What I do remember clearly is that he bought two quarts of black enamel and a new brush, and that early one warm summer morning he began painting the hood, working down from the top hinge, across the side panel, painting carefully around the trim and over the left front fender. Then he did the other side, and slowly worked across the cowl, to the front door, the brush moving in slow, certain strokes, in exactly the same way he worked, with a much smaller brush, to repaint my toy cars as a Christmas surprise.

The sun ascended, the day got hot, and by noon he had more than half the car painted. Then he put the brush in a fruit jar filled with paint thinner and went into the house for lunch, probably a baloney sandwich and java, and smoked a couple of cigarettes. When he came out again the sun blazed against the left side of the car, making the metal so hot you could not leave your finger on it for long, and when the brush hit it the paint flowed.

The odor was overwhelming, but pleasant, warm and welcoming. Years later, when I built model airplanes, the smell of the dope reminded me of the car my father painted in the driveway. Or cars. Perhaps there were others, for I seem to remember reclining in the sloping curve of a front fender, the paint slightly tacky under the summer sun. I do not remember ripples, drips or awkward brush strokes, just the indelible odor of warm metal, freshly painted.

Memories of the World, Circa 1941

I assume that anyone who owns an old car is interested in the time it was built. Relevant information might include the state of the economy, who was president, what songs or motion pictures were popular, which people were prominent, and so on. These facts, which are easily obtainable, fill out the sense of the time period and often have bearing on the car's unique qualities. For example, it might be a rare 1942 model, one of a few hundred built before World War II forced an end to production. Built a decade later, the car no doubt had Korean War chrome. Or it might be one of the first "hardtop convertibles," a truly transitional model between past and future.

But the smaller events, the nuances of daily life, are harder to discern. Sometimes the car can offer a clue. For example, a car that came from the factory without a radio or a heater makes a statement about the economy on national and personal levels. One wonders about the person who bought a car with only one windshield wiper, one sun visor, and one taillight; he could apparently afford a new car but a stripped model. One wonders why he didn't buy a cheaper make or a slightly used car.

One wonders whether he went to the movies on a week night when tickets were cheap, if his wife put a patch on top of a patch on his jeans, if he rolled his own smokes. While there are probably no accurate answers, unless you know the car's original owner, it's necessary to think about such things to understand the car's history. The world has changed so quickly and most of us forget so much about daily life that a car does not need to be truly antique to come from a different time.

For example, my father had only one new car during a lifetime filled with old cars. It was a `41 Chevy coupe that he bought late in the year from Fields Chevrolet in Portland, Oregon. The evening we picked it up I crawled onto the shelf between the back seat and the rear window and rode home that way; oddly, I do not remember anyone yelling at me to get down.

I have many other specific memories because we owned the car nearly seven years, but what comes to mind now is an impression of the time. I do know that in 1935, when my parents came to Portland, they did not own a car—they did not own anything—and my father walked the streets looking for work. But by 1938 they had somehow managed to save enough money to buy a house. It cost $800, and they got it without help from any government agency.

In 1941 my father got a job in the shipyard, the only good job he had in his life. He ran a whirly crane, sitting 100 feet in the air, lifting big pieces of steel from the dock to the ship-in-progress. I don't know what the job paid, but he earned enough to pay the balance on that modest house and for us to afford, for the first time, some amenities. The old wood-burning kitchen range was replaced with a gas stove. We got our first refrigerator in 1941, a Sears

Coldspot, which my mother used for over 30 years. What a remarkable device that was! Before that we had a wooden icebox that depended on a block of ice to cool perishables. We had a metal sign that hung on a nail on the front porch with four numbers on it; if you put the sign out, with a 25 at the top, a man with a wagon or a truck came by and dropped off a 25-lb. block of ice. I clearly remember the delivery service. In hot weather the driver would take an ice pick and break off a chunk of ice for us.

In a year with so many good things happening, it seems natural that we took a vacation that involved a long drive. That trip is the only vacation of any distance or duration that I can remember. Just as we'd drink Kool-Aid rather than soda pop, and have flavored ice cubes rather than Popsicles, a vacation usually meant that my father would drive a short distance out of town, drive up an old logging road, and when we found a clearing we'd pitch a tent for the weekend. We never went far from home, and that was true of other people, too, which is why many older cars were low-mileage vehicles.

My father told people that he knew a war was coming—even if politicians in Washington, D.C. didn't—so he bought a new 1941 Chevrolet, knowing that production would be suspended for the duration, and that fall, a few months before the Japanese bombed Pearl Harbor, we drove to San Francisco. Of necessity, that meant driving south on Highway 101, a twisting two-lane road that had recently been completed. To leave town was a big adventure, in a time when small things, like stopping at a remote gas station for a bottle of cold pop, or staying the night in a motor lodge, mattered.

The next day we got to San Francisco, and Redwood City, where my aunt Jo, my mother's sister, lived. I have no vivid memory of our stay, except that the adults went out for an evening of fun, hitting places like Fisherman's Wharf and Treasure Island, names that seemed to me as exotic as Bombay or Istanbul. I imagine them giddy with the excitement of being in a strange city with a few bucks in their pockets, and that mixture of excitement and

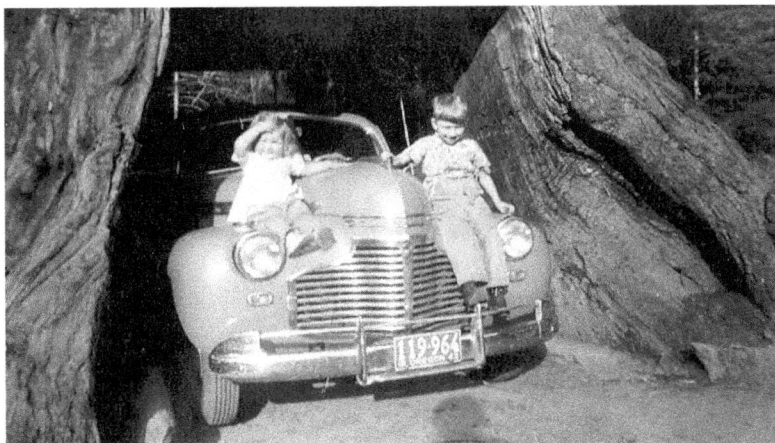

apprehension as another world war loomed closer. The Depression was past, happy times were here again, and the world was changing.

On our return to Portland we drove that narrow highway through the redwoods, a forest primeval and eternal symbol of the West. In addition to the natural wonders, there was an element of hucksterism in blatant roadside attractions, such as the House of Mystery, the Winchester House, and huge trees that were notched so that a car could drive through the trunks.

The Shrine Tree at River Vista Lodge was an estimated 5,000 years old and seemed to have been split by lightning at its base. In those simpler times, such a tree was the equivalent of, say, Disneyland, and there must be a million photographs of cars passing through it. We were fascinated by one of the hollowed-out trees, and my father drove through it, stopping only to photograph the Chevy with my sister and I posed on the front fenders. Then he bought a redwood burl which he brought home and kept watered, with the hope that a redwood tree would grow from it. At the time it did not seem to matter that we would have to wait a hundred years.

Oasis

Why does this illustration make him think of red pop? Maybe Nesbitt, Nehi or something local, like White Rock or Shasta. Some obscure brand, long gone, as far removed from the present as the glass bottle itself.

The soda pop was the promise that his parents had made. If he was good he'd get a bottle of pop when they stopped for gas. He was afraid the promise had been forgotten as time stretched on, like the two-lane road that reached across vast spaces where he did not see even one house. Occasionally a car appeared, a dark hump in the distance, no larger than a bug smashed on the windshield. As he watched, the hump slowly grew in size, reflected light from some shiny surface, took a distinct shape. Then suddenly it was past them.

Such small distractions almost made travel bearable. He searched the landscape for antelope, or even a prairie dog. Hot air came through the side window, open a crack, and the mohair upholstery itched like wool against his skin. They had been driving for days. He longed to get up and walk into another room, or into the backyard, to climb into the hammock and read a

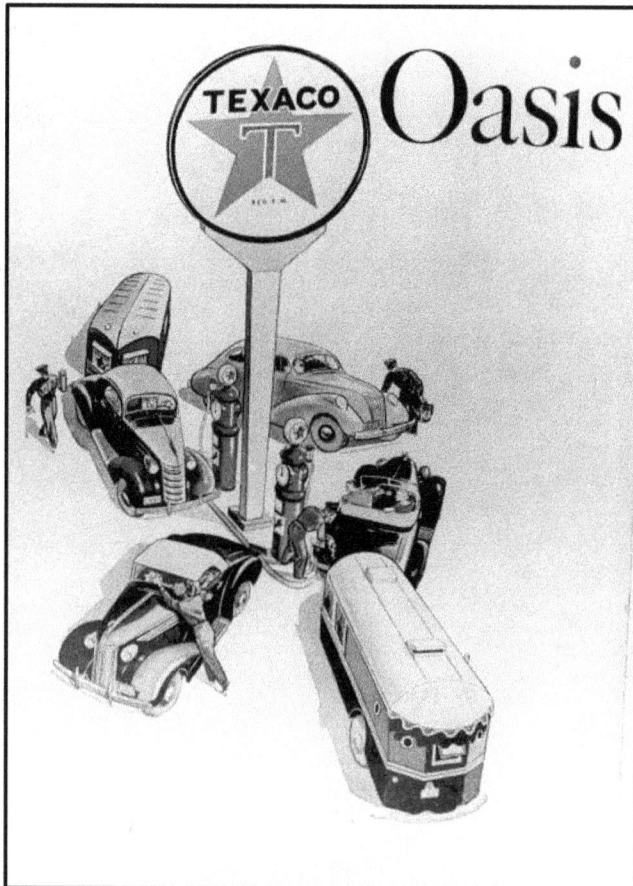

comic book. He longed to be able to go into the kitchen, open the refrigerator and take an aluminum ice cube tray from the small freezing compartment. His mother often poured red Kool-Aid into the tray, and inserted toothpicks for handles.

He heard mutterings from the front seat, and as he looked out the windshield he saw, far in the distance, grain elevators, like three fingers poking skyward. At their bases he knew there would be a town—or at least a gas station, perhaps a small cafe, a place with soda pop. As he thought of the Kool-Aid ice cubes, and the way he could suck the cool color from them, he realized his mouth was as dry as the hot breeze coming in the window. He tried to swallow as the elevators remained in the distance. His mother talked about tuna fish sandwiches for lunch, but all he wanted was soda pop. Time was suspended; the road danced with heat waves, and he thought the grain elevators were a mirage.

Finally the long moment was broken as the car slowed. There was a dusty apron, a spattered sign with a red star, the dry odor of gasoline. An old man rose from the chair outside the door and came up to the car. Beside the chair, in the shade, was the soda pop machine. The boy got out, stretched, then lifted the lid. In the cool water were colored caps, like tiny mushrooms. Coca-Cola, Pepsi, RC, Hires root beer, Squirt, orange pop and red pop. Although he had made up his mind many hot miles ago, his hand hovered over the bottles. His throat longed for the citric taste of Squirt, the sweet pulp of Orange Crush, but he drew out a bottle of red pop and uncapped it on the opener.

Leaning on the corner of the building, where grasshoppers clacked in the dust, he rolled the cool bottle against his cheeks and forehead, then took a small sip. It tasted red like strawberries or cherries, and his throat relaxed. He held the bottle up and light refracted through it, like a prism, creating a hundred small red stars.

A Simplimatic Time

I love this 1941 advertisement for the new DeSoto. Although the illustration is not fine art, it meets my criterion for judging art: is it something I would want to look at on my wall every day? I have to answer yes, primarily because I find it visually interesting and because it so strongly conveys a time period.

It appeared April 7, 1941, exactly eight months before the Japanese bombed Pearl Harbor, sending America into four years of global warfare. From that conflict would come the death of millions of people as well as inventions that otherwise might have been years in the future, such as radar, rockets and pressurized airplanes. The world would never be the same.

But in April, 1941 America enjoyed the innocence and pleasures of this advertisement. I love the use of the primary colors: blue sky, red roof, white house, blue automobile. Details are omitted, for the sake of clarity. There's one tree, two bushes. Although that is a huge house, its lines are broken by only a couple windows lightly sketched. The mountain in the background is a pale monolith. There are no clouds foreshadowing war here; in fact, there is only the hint of white against that vast panoply of blue. This is the stuff of song: my blue heaven, a nest in the west, let the rest of the world go by.

It is set appropriately in the west, probably in California, as suggested by the mountain, the palm tree and the endless blue sky. In the west there was room for a huge house isolated from neighbors, with room to unwind, play tennis on one's own court, have a barbeque on the patio toward dark. All this would be shared with other successful young professionals, who were also glamorous and tanned.

The advertisement answers the question: what kind of car would such people drive? A DeSoto, of course. They are so secure that they do not need a convertible to convey who they are; a conservative, but deluxe, tudor sedan will give their lives flair but it will also blend with the masses. It's a gorgeous car, its robin's egg blue paint and two-tone blue interior accented by the optional white sidewall tires, simple but stylish integrated grille and wider belt and fender trim. The ad cites the advantages of the 105 hp straight-six engine—"the way it whips you out and around other cars"—as well as the "new sturdier box-type frame! New Shockless Steering! New Safety Wheel Rims to keep flat tires from rolling off the wheel."

The big news was hidden: the Fluid Drive with Simplimatic transmission means that the driver does not need to shift gears manually. This device DeSoto compared with other great automotive inventions such as the self-starter and four-wheel hydraulic brakes. Tired from a couple sets of tennis? Drive home in your new DeSoto freed from the chores of shifting gears. The ad reminds us that "You don't have to shift or use the clutch for normal driving." Like the new electric hand mixer, waffle iron and wringer washing machines, the Fluid Drive made life easier. And it's interesting that in the early ads it was called a Simplimatic transmission, because very soon the world would become complex, even chaotic.

Things We Loved Too Much

Men have grown old and wondered how as boys they began a life-long love affair with machines. While individual answers might vary, we need to look at the one thing all internal combustion engines have in common: exhaust gasses. We were all seduced at a tender age by the beautiful odor of exhaust!

A tune-up, or even a routine checkup, required you to place your palm against the tailpipe opening, to feel the regular beat of the engine. Exhaust was deflected upward; it was impossible to not breathe the honey-sweet smoke, but no one complained. There was the excitement and almost uncontained joy that the engine was running, like a promise of future mobility.

In the garage, exhaust was soon visible, gathering in layers like cumulus clouds, filling even the smallest spaces, but there was no hurry, no sense of urgency; not until you had the carburetor adjusted and the timing set did you push open the garage doors, where the chilly air cleared away cobwebs in the brain.

No one told us, there was no warning label anywhere, but if they had, would we have listened? Of course, in those days exhaust odor was different, more pleasant, even with or perhaps because of tetraethyl lead additives. That's why we were also seduced by the odor of gasoline. That's why we hung around service stations, and that's why we worked in them, even hoped to someday own one. As gasoline junkies, we wanted to be near the source.

We were intoxicated by the thick, pleasant smell of hydraulic brake fluid. Also the odor of engine oil, and transmission fluid so red it might have come from pomegranates. Also the odor of oil hitting a hot exhaust manifold, or two stroke exhaust.

To enter a commercial garage on Monday morning, after it had been closed all weekend, was to drink in the machine cocktail, a melding of cutting oils, a hint of acetylene, the solvent used to clean the cement floor. One entered, and breathed deeply; it was not recklessness but romance. There was something reassuring in the air, a reminder that there was work to do, and that this was where it would get done.

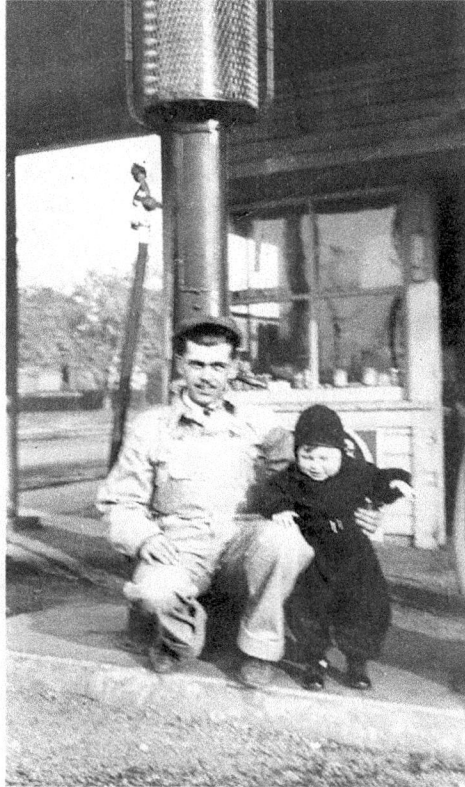

Alberts Drake, father and son, in the fall of 1936. This gas station was located at 59th and Foster, within walking distance from his home. Note the old gravity feed gasoline pump

Foto Review

Imagine a world where automotive activities went underground, new car production and races were halted, and auto-related publications nearly were.

Such was the case during World War II. You couldn't buy a new car or attend an auto race from 1942-45, and the only place you could read about them would be the odd article in *Popular Mechanics*, or an issue of *The Motor* if it crossed the pond.

To meet this need, *National Speed Sport News*, which had nothing to report anyway, brought out three issues of *Foto Review Auto Racing Album* between 1943-45. They were about 30 pages long and were not identical in size, perhaps due to paper shortages. The eclectic content was limited to photos and short captions.

The photos showed pre-war midgets, big cars and road races in places like Argentina. There were photos of race track owners such as Frank Funk, promoters like the Lavelys and race car drivers. Most of the drivers have been forgotten, but there were shots of Walk Faulkner and Cal Niday early in their careers.

The unnamed editor of the second volume wrote that the publication was "a special feature widely requested by our Auto Racing Sportsmen…It is most valued at this time when auto racing is suspended due to war restrictions. We hope it affords racing enthusiasts keen pleasure to look over old landmarks and old racing scenes…reminding you of the good old former racing days."

A third and final volume was published May 1945, about three months before the war ended and car production and auto racing resumed once again.

What we wanted: something like this Bowles Seal Fast Special, which Rex Mays drove to the pole position in the 1940 Indy 500 race.

What we got:...not! No one I knew could afford a gas-powered tether car. These guys appear to be 30 years old, at least.

Cars and Comics

Cars, comics and kids naturally go together; most of us got our early ideas about cars from the examples in comic books and comic strips. Those cars ranged from realistic to absurd, depending upon the artist's vision and draftsmanship. Since the cars existed only on paper they did not need to be functional, and that appealed to our young minds. They could be low, streamlined and fast. They could do incredible things; the Green Hornet's Black Beauty could emit clouds of an incapacitating gas. They were, in fact,

the opposite of the kinds of cars our fathers drove.

It's appropriate that the cover of the first original comic book, *Action*, issue number one (1938), should feature a car. It's the first appearance of Superman and to show his strength he lifts a car overhead and smashes it into a huge rock, while the crooks flee. The car is a new 1937 Ford sedan, and the drawing is fairly realistic, although young readers were no doubt more impressed by the figure of Superman. (Fifteen years later that same pose and situation was used on the cover of *Action*, issue number thirty-three (1953). The artists knew a good thing, even though Superman's strength had long been established.)

A car that stands out in my mind was the touring used in the popular funny paper strip, "Harold Teen". The car was covered with sayings such as "Hop in, sis" and "Capacity 6 gals". I suspect that the car imitated one the artist had seen on the street, and the comic strip car no doubt inspired many teenagers to paint funny sayings on their jalopies.

Another unique car was the one used in "Smokey Stover", a zany strip. This vehicle was a caricature of a car, and was memorable because it had only two wheels! It also had writing on the sides, crazy sayings; the words changed all the time but an example I remember was "Notary Sojac"!

Cops had cars, crooks had cars, even cowboys had cars. Cars allowed the comics to show chases and crashes, as well as lovers parked under a full moon. Perhaps part of the appeal cars in the comics had was due to the fact that many people during the 1930s and 1940s did not own a car.

That `41 Chevy Meant Something to Mom

"Everyone has owned, or knows someone who has owned, a 1941 Chevrolet." I don't remember who wrote that line but when I read it, years ago, it seemed true. The 1941 Chevrolet was a popular car: it was nicely styled, had nice appointments, and it seemed sleeker, larger and more integrated than previous models. When I was in high school in the 1950s I knew a couple guys who had 1940 Chevys and a semi-friend, Bob Feeley, had a 1941 Chevy coupe with whitewalls and dual pipes. Bob's `41 seemed like a more mature car when compared with the `40 Chevys, with their bolt-on headlights and stubby bodies. Chevrolet's 1941 models were desirable machines throughout the 1950s and 1960s, and still are today, although their rarity belies their prewar popularity.

Whenever I do see a 1941 Chevrolet I'm reminded that a `41 was the only new car my father ever owned. What I remember about the car comes from memory, family folklore and whatever a child can infer from long-ago adult conversations. In 1941, after a series of hit-and-miss WPA jobs, my father got a good job in the shipyards, the only good job he ever had. Perhaps it was the nature of the job, but he felt that America would soon be at war, so he thought it'd be a good idea to buy a new car—something that would last for the duration.

He bought a brand-new 1941 Chevrolet club coupe, a car several inches lower than his 1935 Packard 120 sedan. That Chevy not only was new, it looked like the car of the future! Although it was tan, the dullest color he could have chosen, it was beautiful. I still remember the ride home from the dealer, Fields Chevrolet; it was night, and I climbed onto the shelf between the back seat and the rear window and felt a mixture of excitement and pure contentment.

In those days, getting a new car was an event. The neighbors came over to look at it, and people talked to my father in gas stations, asking questions and looking under the hood. Ours was a lower-class neighborhood, and most of the families had cars from the 1920s and 1930s. In 1941 we also got our first refrigerator, a Sears Coldspot, and we replaced the wood burning kitchen stove with a new gas range. My mother, who knew nothing about cars, and who never drove during her life, was as proud of that new car in the driveway as she was of the new appliances in her kitchen. She was conscious of our economic status, and faced with shiny new devices she no doubt thought that we'd been elevated several notches in the social structure. She loved that car, not for what it was, but for what it represented.

As I recall, shortly after he bought the Chevy, my father thought we ought to take a trip in it, before gas was rationed. I think it was in August or September, just months before Pearl Harbor, that we drove down the coast on Highway 101, a road that had been finished a few years earlier. My mother brought along a huge pot of stew, and when we stopped for the night in a "motor lodge," as motels were called, she heated the stew for our dinner. Of that trip I recall two things: savoring a bottle of red pop at a gas station in the middle of nowhere, and listening to the "Red Ryder" program on the car radio as dusk fell on the ocean off to the right.

The next trip I recall was in 1945, when my mother's mother was dying in North Dakota, and we tried to get there before she died. My father drove with urgency, whipping that car over the mountains and across the long plains of Montana. I think I felt anxious and concerned about my grandmother, but I also felt immense boredom—I thought we'd never arrive.

My father had an old sedan that he drove to the shipyards during the war, and perhaps the Chevrolet sat at home most of the time. But it did not remain immaculate. One night my father came home from somewhere and the car's grille was smashed in. Someone had stopped quickly, he said. Now, fifty years later, I suspect he'd been drinking that night. I've forgotten how he got the serious dent in the left rear fender, but I remember the dent.

After the war he personally felt the nation's sense of optimism, and he and a partner started a construction company. They worked awfully hard, but I suspect most of the money went back into the steam shovel, the gasoline shovel and the dump trucks that were constantly breaking down. My father seemed able to do anything, but, in retrospect, I now wonder whether he always knew what he was doing. On one occasion when he was blasting he ordered us to move back to a safe distance. He dropped the plunger on the detonator, the ground rose into a cloud, and within seconds huge rocks were falling from the sky and at least a couple landed on the Chevrolet's hood and roof.

One day in 1948 he came home in a big, black 1942 Lincoln-Zephyr four-door sedan. I was beginning to get interested in cars and, fickle youth, I loved this "new" car. It had push button doors, a spotlight, an ivory-colored steering wheel, underseat heaters front and rear and an immense back seat. My father had had the dealer install a brand-new `49 Ford V-8 engine in the space where that V-12 had been, and that made the car even more interesting, I thought.

One might suppose that my mother would view the Lincoln as another step up the class ladder, but she threw a fit. She remembered the Chevy the way it had been seven years before; it represented something to her, and she wanted it back. We all got in that huge Lincoln and drove on Sandy and Union avenues, streets lined with used car dealers' lots, searching for that dented, dust-colored old Chevy. I suspect that my father was quietly laughing as he pretended to look; perhaps even avoided the lot where it sat. But my sister and I were dutiful children, eager to please, and we looked intently at the rows of used cars under the bright pennants, hoping to placate our screaming mother, but we never saw the Chevy again.

1942 Mercury

The issue of *Life* magazine published just days before the December 7, 1941 strike against Pearl Harbor by Japan had the theme "Air Power" and displayed on its cover a close-up photo of the updated B-17 bomber. While other ads hinted at the possibility of America entering the war, citing the need to buy a fuel-efficient car (Oldsmobile) and one that would last longer than an impending war (Plymouth), the advertisement for the new 1942 Mercury emphasized the car's virtues by comparing it with the new airplanes. These were not commercial planes either, but U.S. Army fighters and bombers. Since the war had not yet begun for America, it was war by association emphasizing the positive elements of engineering and industry.

The headline read, "Like Uncle Sam's Newest Planes, Mercury Has More Power Per Pound!" Mercury had been introduced as a marque only three years earlier and there was a need to keep it distinct from Ford models. The phrase "airplane-engineered" was often used by the factory to characterize the Mercury. "You'll thrill to the Style, Economy, and surging power of this new and different airplane-engineered car!" said the ad, indicating that its difference offered both speed and economy! This was achieved because "Mercury is Airplane-Engineered—Like the new Army planes, it is streamlined from core to outward lines, free from excess weight, and has more power per pound than most other cars."

The Mercury's 100 horsepower V-8 versus the Ford's 85 horsepower V-8 helped to make the distinction between the two marques. The nearly identical suspensions were separated by Mercurys "sky-ride", which was possible because of the "longer, slow-motion springs and improved shock absorbers. And Mercury combines a lower center of gravity with wider tread."

In late 1941 the message was that we should be prepared for a possible global war and so should a new car buyer. The actuality of combat was played down. To show that Mercury is streamlined there is a rendering of stylized American bombers against a sunrise. Another rendering shows an officer taking a photograph of a fellow officer and wife in their 1942 Mercury convertible. The dominant central rendering shows a woman in a new two-door Mercury sedan talking with a man, perhaps her husband, who is suited up—complete with parachute—and ready for a pre-dawn flight in his A.A.F. fighter. Along with the military aspect, there is a domestic element: should there be a war, here is a woman, and a car, to come home to.

To soften the war angle, there are animals in the ad. These include a pheasant in flight to show streamlining, a greyhound to represent speed and a hippopotamus to indicate the car's roominess. At the bottom is an eagle, to remind us of Mercury's motto, "The Aviation Idea in Automobiles", and also of America's and Ford Motor Company's contribution to the war effort:

"Built to serve the U.S.—Reconnaissance cars . . . airplane engines . . . complete bombers and tanks . . ."

Too soon America would be involved in a global war that would need those military machines and Mercury production would halt, with a total of fewer than 25,000 cars built for the 1942 model year.

The Home Front

This episode of Dudley Fisher's comic strip, "Right Around Home," titled "Spring Tune-Up!" is my favorite. It was published in a Sunday paper dated April 27, 1941. In a single frame it shows Otto working on his old car, and about twenty family members and neighbors offering comments or playing tricks on the mechanic.

A child gets greasy playing with a car part, a woman (perhaps his wife) wants him to repair her carpet sweeper, a neighbor wants to take a part to use as a fishing weight, four of Otto's friends are going to confuse him by adding extra parts, a neighbor woman watches the parts coming off the engine and is reminded of her operation, a wife sees that Otto will need a new car and reminds her husband of this potential sale, etc. Even the birds and the dogs offer comments. In the lower right hand corner two young couples are having a mild argument, and although this activity seems separate from the car repair scene it's on the same theme of trickery.

The car is a generic early 1930s two-door sedan with a four-cylinder flathead engine, although the radiator seems to date from the 1920s. It doesn't need to be more specific. Although the kibitzer on the left said that Otto began the project simply to find a squeak, it was common to tackle an extensive job on a weekend. The engines were fairly simple, and one required only basic tools in order to dismantle them.

So this common activity is a catalyst to bring the other characters into the story. In other episodes the catalyst would be a Halloween prank, a neighborhood tiff, or an outdoor barbeque—anything to get a bunch of people into the story's moment. That sense of community is what I like best about the strip.

I can dimly remember April, 1941, or a span of time about then anyway, and I'm certain that in those halcyon days before Pearl Harbor and our involvement in World War II, my family and our neighbors did have a sense of community. Our house still had a wide front porch, as did our neighbors' houses, and we spent a lot of time there during nice weather. Neighbors wandered over, the kids started playing tag or kickball, the women exchanged recipes and gossip, and the men wandered into the driveway to lean on the family car. The hood was raised, the engine started, and each man offered an opinion. It was a meeting place not very different from the village square, but it does not seem to happen much anymore.

At the bottom is a single strip, a coda to the larger frame. The four friends pulled a prank on Otto by adding parts that they had found at a junkyard, hoping to confuse him with the leftover parts. In the lower strip we learn that the trick backfired—Otto used the parts they supplied and that they could have sold for $7.

There's something so just and good-natured about that small addition, and without it we would still laugh but there would be less humor. As readers, we want Otto to triumph—before dark.

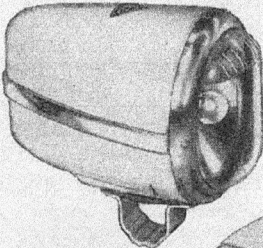
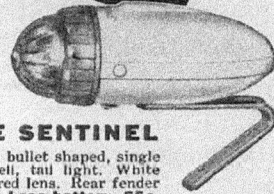

Blitz Buggy

The postmark on this card is Oct. 28, 1941, roughly five weeks before the Japanese bombed Pearl Harbor. My uncle Chuck sent it from Denver, en route to Texas, to his mother who was staying with us in Portland. He was in the 8th Air Force in England for the duration. In this way the war separated families. The caption on this postcard is interesting: "Reconnaissance Car (Blitz Buggy) and Motorcycle Trooper".

Rationing

For most of World War II, from 1942 to 1945, car owners were forced to limit their driving because gasoline and tires were rationed.

At first the government ordered service stations to close early to reduce consumption, but by 1942 rationing went into effect as did a national speed limit of 35 mph. A car owner got a sticker for the windshield, indicating that he had A, B, or C priorities depending on how important he was to the war effort; the majority had an A sticker, which, with the correct coupons, allowed drivers only five gallons of gas a week. If one had an essential job, such as war work, or a profession such as a doctor, one was entitled to more than five gallons a week. (Various politicians, including members of Congress, got an X sticker, which allowed them unlimited gasoline.)

Gasoline shortages were real, but part of the reason it was rationed was

to save tires, which were almost impossible to find. Tubes were patched, suitable tires could be recapped, but those mounted on the car were driven beyond reason. Tires not being used were "donated" to the government. Although synthetic rubber was being developed, the shortage extended to other rubber products such as hot water bottles, shower curtains and footwear.

At war's end it seemed true that gasoline was available while tires remained scarce. A small article in the August 14, 1945 *Oregon Journal* noted " There's plenty of gasoline in the huge Portland terminal storage tanks for that long overdue vacation...when Office and Price Administration lifts gasoline rationing." Officials expected that one tanker a day would arrive in

Portland from California, and each tanker carried three million gallons of gasoline. A delay of two weeks between V-J Day and the end of rationing would allow the gas to be distributed to all stations.

That same article noted that "The travel 'bottleneck' in the months ahead will be tires, not gasoline, and there's no indication as to when the rubber supply will be sufficient to lift rationing. WPB (War Production Board) has warned the public not to be overly optimistic concerning the availability of new tires." In a separate news brief, it was noted that the OPA would lift rationing on used truck tires on August 17th, and that it planned to "allow unrationed sale of passenger tires made from reclaimed rubber." A smaller story noted that "The Office of Surplus Property is arranging to sell new airplane tires and tubes...(for) farm machinery, passenger cars, trucks, and farm wagons..."

However, they would be sold only to tire manufacturers, wholesalers, and dealers. That might mean that the family automobile would stay on blocks in the garage for a while longer, which was one reason so many low mileage cars were available in later years.

Riding Bike

On Christmas morning, 1943, my father sent me to a neighbor's house on a pretext, and when I returned the first thing I saw was the bicycle beside the Christmas tree. I was thrilled beyond words. We'd already opened our presents—I got a leather billfold, a ball, a book, a game, and so on—and I had not expected anything more, least of all a bicycle. For one thing, there was a war on and bikes were hard to get. This bike, a Western Flyer, had been owned by the boy next door, Steve Weber, who had joined the merchant Marine and my father had bought it from his parents for, I think, $23.00. Also, although I wanted a bike, I was too young.

That soon became apparent. On the street my father lifted me to the seat and with my leg stretched to its limit, my foot could barely touch the high pedal. He held me up, kept the bike steady and ran beside it, urging me to push down on the pedal. I could not. When my father released the bike I coasted for only a few feet before it began to fall and he caught it.

But for those few feet I had been mobile!

I remember that after a long, desperate period of trying, of feeling that I would never be able to maintain my balance, steer and pedal simultaneously, one day I could. My father would get me started, run beside me as I pushed down, got the pedals to rotate, then caught the other pedal at its apex, and then he'd help me slow the bike and dismount. Soon I could do all that without him.

Well, almost. I could not get on the bike and get it going by myself. The telephone pole closest to the house had a support pole, perhaps twelve feet tall, and one day I mustered up the courage to lean my bike against them. I remember the day was warm so perhaps I'd spent five months learning to ride. I climbed up the bike, swung a leg over the seat and, gritting my teeth, I

got one pedal to the top and pushed off. The bike wobbled, then straightened out. When the other pedal came to the top I searched, looked down, found it and, wobbling, pedaled again, moving forward. There were no curbs, driveway cuts or sidewalks that I might run into, and so I moved more or less smoothly down the street, which was oiled gravel. Beyond the house next to ours that rudimentary pavement ended, and from there on the road was dirt, with twin ruts and serious mud puddles. Even in summer, when the puddles had dried up, the road was a collection of bumps. But this also meant that there was almost no traffic on my street, so I could weave and wander on the bike without worrying about cars.

In fact, as I knew when I got on the bike, the only thing I had to worry about was how to get off. I kept riding, sometimes for an hour or more, pedaling back and forth in front of the house, delaying the moment when I would have to stop. The gravel was sharp, like a kitchen grater, and I tried to not think about what it would do to my skin. Finally, when I had to stop to go to the bathroom, I rode as slowly as possible, swung my right leg back off, let go of the handlebars then jumped, ran beside the bike for a few feet and watched, with real misgivings, as it fell over with a crash.

I grew; I mastered the machine. I was able to mount it myself, move forward, swing my right leg over, straddle the bar and pump, all the while keeping my balance. It seemed to take forever to reach that point, and I'm told that once learned one never forgets. And I'm sure that everyone who grew up riding a bike remembers the time when he was allowed to circle the block, then the experience of riding two, perhaps three city blocks. Suddenly one's concept of the world changed; it became bigger. I was free to roam, alone, the larger area we called the neighborhood. Over time I went beyond the busier streets, to the park or a friend's house.

That sense of independence and pleasure depended on the wheel.

In the summer I rode my bike back and forth on the street by my house before breakfast, and after I rode around the neighborhood, until I knew every rise and fall by heart. Ramona was the only street with a sidewalk, and I cruised it for hours, up one side and down the other, a distance of five city blocks.My bike was original except for two additions. On the back fender was a flat piece of metal, chrome plated, with a reflector. It was shaped like an eagle, and stamped B.F. Goodrich. I loved that bird, and cried when someone took it. I've seen a couple at swap meets in recent years, but they were priced at a sum that was more than I wanted to pay. The other extra was also a pre-war accessory, a pair of leather guards, lined with fleece, that fit over the handlebar grips for warmth. In cold weather they made me feel wonderful, but, unfortunately, the first day I rode my bike to Lents school one was stolen. My area of Portland which is called Lents, had its share of scumbags and scallywags then, and it's 100 times worse now. Lents is called Felony Flats by the police. Today the scumbags in Lents would steal the bike!

Because of the thugs in Lents I never got any other accessories, although I was always looking at them in catalogs and stores. I coveted various lights, especially the sleek, streamlined designs, either painted or chromed, that seemed to belong on the fenders of a fast car. I wanted an electric horn, something that would announce my presence and warn pedestrians. The problem was that those lights and horn required batteries, and we never seemed to have any. So I looked in catalogues for a generator, the kind that tips in to rub against the tire to generate power. I wanted a chrome-plated rear view mirror, possibly two; a speedometer; handgrips in a color other than black; a cushy seat and much more.

I never even added reflectors, the easiest and more inexpensive addition. It wasn't like I didn't have time; I rode that bike for nearly ten years. I rode it everywhere, to school, to the Saturday matinee at the Aero Theater, to Johnson Creek, on trails at a nearby stone quarry and up a nearby mountain, Mt. Scott. In the summer of 1950 Jimmy Strand and I, armed with our .22 pistols and rifles, sleeping bags and camping gear, rode to the Government Camp level of Mt. Hood.

The year is 1949, the month is April; the Japanese Plum trees are in blossom and the day is pleasantly warm. It was Bonnie's birthday, and this year she got a new bicycle complete with headlight and tail lights, horn, rack, skirt guard, whitewall tires and two-tone paint. She looks pleased as punch, but I look miffed. Am I jealous? Is it because I have stripped down my Western Flyer for racing? Check out the Schwinn knee-action front fork that my father adapted to that old beater! Behind us is my father's 1942 Lincoln Zephyr sedan, and in the far background is that 1934 Terraplane.

The only thing I added was a playing card held to the front fork by a wooden clothespin; as the wheel revolved the spokes rubbed against the card, and the sound was very like a gasoline engine. It made terrific sound, even at slow speeds, and it must have driven people crazy. But I was told the card

would soon loosen the spokes, so I got rid of it.

The reason, or reasons, I didn't add accessories was because, first, I didn't have the money, and second, I rode my bike in a manner that would've ripped off those doo-dads. When I dug out I came down hard on the right pedal, spinning the tire and shouting, "Scratch gravel!" like a cowboy movie star. I rode it fast. I rode it up and down the hill in Lents Park, and through a wooded area near my school, where the dirt path was packed hard. That path had a couple high places which we took at speed, launching our bikes into the air. I'd ride quickly across the school playground, then jam the pedal back, locking the rear wheel and throwing the bike into a slide. Later, with practice, we began doing that on the sidewalk in Lents; we loved being reckless.

The most reckless thing we did was to ride our bicycles on the motorcycle trails at Indian Rock. This was an abandoned quarry, only blocks from my house, and motorcycle riders had used it for years, creating a network of trails. The highest point was about a hundred feet above the quarry floor, but some of the trails went nearly straight up. My friend, Jimmy Strand, and I went to Indian Rock all the time, in all kinds of weather, and while there were a couple hills we could not navigate, in other areas, going downhill, we could go as fast as a motorcycle.

A bumpy road led into the quarry, and the most obvious trail went from the road to the top of the highest rock. The trail was wide, with a level area of a few feet midway, so a motorcyclist could make a running start, scoot up the first section, take a deep breath and slide his weight back for traction and crank it on. At the top there was a space about 20 feet in circumference where he could turn around; beyond that was a cliff, straight down. Anyone could make it up the first half. The second half was more difficult: it was steeper, with a deep groove and nowhere to go but up. Those who didn't make it to the top might be able to stop, lay the bike over and, often with help, get it back to the flat spot in the middle. The unlucky ones went over backward, or saw their cycle flip-flop down the incline to the rocks below, the engine roaring when the throttle stuck.

Jimmy and I couldn't possibly ride our bicycles up the hill, so we dragged them over halfway, then jumped on and shot downward. Think about it: a motorcycle had a kill button or a compression release, so that the dead engine would slow the machine's descent. We had only the rear wheel brake, which, once applied, made the bike slide one way or the other. When the hill was muddy the brake was useless. At the bottom the trail flattened out, then rose at the dirt road, and under the best conditions we'd hit that bump, shooting skyward and landing twenty feet away. On one occasion I came down fast, hit that bump, went into the air and the bike landed on the front wheel; I shot forward, still gripping the handlebars, riding on the crossbar, my crotch against the forks. The landing was painful!

By this time I'd stripped the bike of its fenders and chain guard, to give it a racing appearance. That was a poor move, since the unguarded chain rubbed grease on my pants leg and the tires threw water and mud on my front and back. I had two paper routes, and loaded fifty or sixty pounds of papers on the bike almost every day. I rode summer and winter, on blistering hot days and on windy, chilling days, and a few times when we had snow. I rode it on dark, unpaved streets when I longed for any kind of headlight. Except for an occasional flat tire, the bike never let me down.

WASHING MACHINE MOTOR POWERS BICYCLE

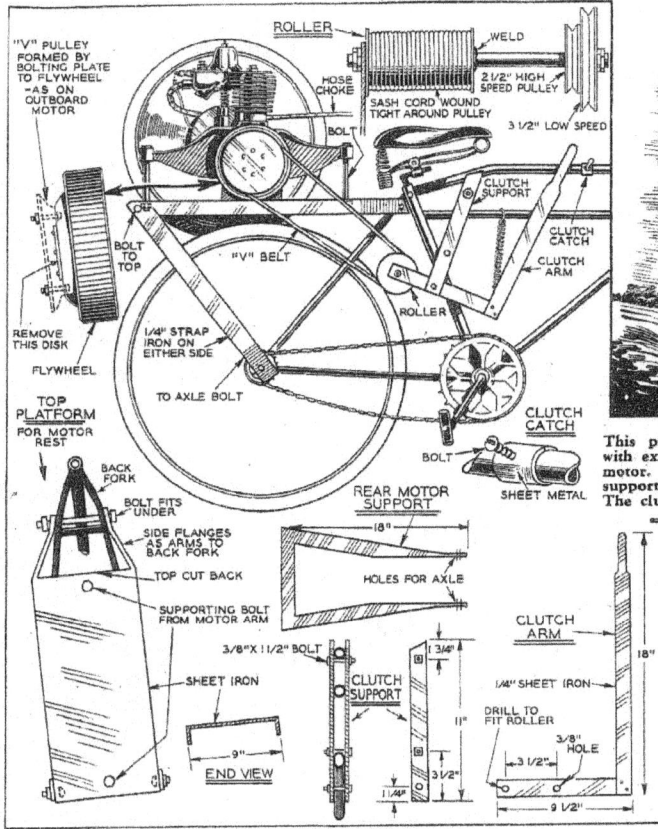

"V" PULLEY FORMED BY BOLTING PLATE TO FLYWHEEL —AS ON OUTBOARD MOTOR

ROLLER

WELD

HOSE CHOKE

SASH CORD WOUND TIGHT AROUND PULLEY

2 1/2" HIGH SPEED PULLEY

3 1/2" LOW SPEED

BOLT

CLUTCH SUPPORT

CLUTCH CATCH

CLUTCH ARM

BOLT TO TOP

"V" BELT

1/4" STRAP IRON ON EITHER SIDE

ROLLER

REMOVE THIS DISK

FLYWHEEL

TO AXLE BOLT

TOP PLATFORM FOR MOTOR REST

BACK FORK

BOLT FITS UNDER

SIDE FLANGES AS ARMS TO BACK FORK

TOP CUT BACK

SUPPORTING BOLT FROM MOTOR ARM

SHEET IRON

3/8"X 1 1/2" BOLT

CLUTCH SUPPORT

9"

END VIEW

BOLT

REAR MOTOR SUPPORT

SHEET METAL

CLUTCH CATCH

18"

HOLES FOR AXLE

1 3/4"

11"

3 1/2"

1/4"

CLUTCH ARM

1/4" SHEET IRON

DRILL TO FIT ROLLER

3/8" HOLE

3 1/2"

9 1/2"

18"

This practical motorbike may be constructed with excellent results using a washing machine motor. Make motor carrier from galvanized iron supported by a frame made of 1/4" strap iron. The clutch arm and support are also cut from this material. A machine bolt serves to hold the clutch arm in place. Set the gas control on the motor until the maximum speed is found. Once set the motor needs no further attention. To stop the bicycle simply throw out the clutch and apply the coaster brake. A two-speed pulley connects from the clutch to motor giving a choice of either high or low speed. In winding the tractive surface on the wheel drive pulley be sure that you wind the rope in the proper direction. Applying shellac to the drum of the pulley before putting on the rope will insure a lasting surface. Besides offering good traction the rope reduces wear on the rear 'tire. In starting out apply the clutch lever gently and pedal at the same time so as to gradually increase momentum.

However, it was getting worn. I think that bike had a built-in knee action, or perhaps the bearings in the cone were worn out, because when I put my weight on the handlebars the front wheel would move outward a couple inches. Something had to be done. I don't remember whose idea it was, but I went to Foster Sporting Goods and for $14.50 bought a brand new Schwinn knee-action front end. It was chrome and black, while the rest of the bike was blue and silver, but to me it was like owning a real Schwinn bike, which I always considered top of the line. The spring fork softened all the bumps on the road, and helped considerably on the trails. The bike felt tight and new; it was my first modified machine.

I loved that bike—it was such a big part of my boyhood—but eventually I let it down. I rode it when I was sixteen, to various wrecking yards in search of car parts. But somewhere along the line I must have felt I was too old to ride a bicycle—better to have my peers see me walking or riding the bus—and I parked it. In the late 1950s or early 1960s a neighbor lady wanted it and I gave it to her. Otherwise, I would probably still have it; if so, I'd treat it like an old friend, with whom I enjoyed and endured much.

The Beautiful and the Banal

Two photographs a couple pages apart in a 1948 college yearbook say more to me about the ideal and the real, about the lofty and the mundane, about the nature of beauty, than anything I've seen recently. Seeing these pictures reminded me of what I had yearned for, what most young men in those days dreamed of, and what we had to settle for.

The 1947 Buick convertible is brand new. It might have come directly from the showroom floor or, more likely, some lucky guy has owned it long enough to bolt on the shiny stuff. It has dual spot lights and a pair of long chrome horns, which, if you squint, recall the massive classics of a decade earlier. It also has dual mirrors, and if the photo weren't cropped, we'd probably see a pair of fog lights in front of the grille, white-wall tires and some kind of full wheel covers.

This is exactly the car I drew on my school notebooks in 1948. I added a couple antennas—with fox tails—but I thought even a stock `46-`48 Buick was the most gorgeous car. One thing I loved about them was the way that the front fender swooped from the headlight down and back to the rear fender. The Buick was the only American car to do this (it was picked up later on the Jaguar XK-120, and appeared on various special-bodied foreign cars). Other American cars of the period had fenders that came back to the middle of the front door, either as a pontoon or a fade-away design, but no other used the Buick design. Because the Buick was a long car, this fender treatment was not only appropriate, but stunning. I'm reasonably certain that when I drew my idealized versions of the Buick I knew girls would be interested (even though I was years away from either a driver's license or dating), as the young woman in the photo, described as the school's first "Homecoming Queen," certainly is. The car is circling the perimeter of a football field during a break in the game. The faces of the driver and the guy in back are obscured, but in my imagination I'm one of them, probably the driver, and although it's fall, with long shadows on the playing field, the chill so apparent that the queen has to wear a coat, the convertible top is down, as I would have it.

If the new Buick convertible was what I wanted, the 1934 Ford five-window coupe was closer to what most of us got as soon as we could drive. Many of them looked like this, with a piece of sheet metal serving as a left rear fender! It wasn't that the owner wanted a fenderless hot rod, he just couldn't find a fender, or the five bucks to buy a fender. So, he has his license plate bolted to the body beside the trunk lid, and the original spare is still on. It might have a radio, or at least it has an antenna—the latter was not necessarily a guarantee of the former.

Joe College is emerging through the driver's window either because the door won't open, or because he's goofing off for the photographer. He seems to have the boundless energy of youth, as seen in his expression and clothes: athletic warm-up jacket, Levis with wide cuffs, argyle socks, and muddy brogues. He might have been in the service during World War II and is now in college on the G.I. Bill. Perhaps he's mimicking a leap he's made before from a wounded airplane or ship.

Or perhaps it's a symbolic leap into the future, into the good job, into the driver's seat of a new Buick.

A Winter's Tale

I recently saw a 1934 Hudson Terraplane (literally "flat earth"!) and I was reminded of the time, over 60 years ago, when I helped my father get one home. At least, in retrospect, I like to think I was helpful.

I'm not sure why I've always remembered that evening or that car. It was not notable, just an old coupe with faded, dark blue paint, one of a long string of old cars that my father got and then got rid of, usually by trading stuff. I have no idea who my father got the car from or where it went. It sat in our driveway for months, perhaps a year, and that I remember because by then I had begun to feel mechanical stirrings and would go out and sit in the coupe, pretending to drive it. That was a change in my attitude from a few months earlier when we first got the car and my father tried to talk with me about engines—mini-lectures about theory and practice—but I refused to listen. I felt uncomfortable, I guess, as a grown-up talked about a grown-up subject. Amazingly, I had almost no interest in cars then; I loved guns and hunting and probably would have been perfectly happy to spend my life in a world without cars.

I also can't recall how we got to the car, but we must have driven because my father brought along some tools and a glass gallon jug of gasoline. I do recall that it was early evening, but already dark with the darkness of winter and a cold wind blew newspapers down the street. My father tinkered with the Terraplane's engine, not bothering to explain anything to me and, while I waited, I moved from one foot to the other, the cold seeping into my bones. I was impatient and eager to be home lying on the floor of that warm front room and listening to a radio drama.

My father poured gas from the jug into the carburetor, pressed the cork back in, and shut the Terraplane's hood. When he got inside, I did too, seeking shelter from that cold wind. The coupe's musty odor increased as we settled on the seat. My father bent over, hands working under the dashboard, his breath raspy, and then there was a spark as he brought two wires together. Some 60 years later I might be tempted to compare that spark with the moment God's finger touched Adam's in Michelangelo's painting on the ceiling of the Sistine Chapel, or Prometheus bringing fire to man, but at that moment it was simply a spark, evidence that there was some juice in the battery. And yet, it must have been more than that. If not, this piece would be titled "1934 Terraplane." That spark hinted at warmth, the genesis of life. And in duration it was unusual; in memory the spark illuminated the coupe's cockpit for a long second so that I can still see the dashboard, steering column and wheel, and my father's face, whisker stubble, his black hair falling forward, and fingers holding the two wires. A person walking past might have seen the two of us within that tiny cockpit, the highlights of our faces illuminated against the darkness, like figures in, say, Van Gogh's "Potato

Eaters" series. Something dark, the interplay between light and dark, the subtle chiaroscuro. We were two males, up to something, perhaps examining a diamond or delivering a baby, fit subjects for a painting.

But we were simply trying to get an old car home. The battery cranked the starter, then quickly lost power. OK, my father said, tapping the accelerator a couple times and getting out to push. I reluctantly got out, shut the door, and pushed, my hands against the cold metal of the trunk lid. Slowly it rolled forward and gained speed. I was thirteen years old and not very strong, but I pushed. My father opened the door and jumped in. As he let out the clutch, the car jerked and slowed. We did that two or three times until I was panting, but then the engine caught. I ran for the door—a suicide door that cut the air like a knife—and struggled to get inside. The engine threatened to stop, but my father kept it running until it smoothed out.

Many cars from the 1930s did not have heaters and the Terraplane might have been one of them. But I do remember heat coming from somewhere—perhaps through extra holes in the firewall. Before my father put the car in gear, the cold was outside. Inside there was the odor of exhaust, blowby, warm rubber, and dry, heated air. As we moved slowly forward my father turned on the lights and the dash was illuminated. I could see the edges of his face, his expression, and, although I didn't know what he was thinking, he seemed happy to be mobile.

Did I think about mortality or a radio program I wanted to hear? I like to think that both of us felt the closeness of the small cockpit's warmth as we moved like pilots through the darkness of the night.

A Vintage Automotive Accessory We'll Never See Again

During the 1940s and 1950s, it seemed that most people smoked cigarettes and auto smoking accessories were very much in vogue at that time.

In 1949, I bought my father three matching accessories made out of blue plastic for his 1942 Lincoln Zephyr. They were a hood-ornament bug deflector, a tray that fit on the dashboard and a hold-all rack that clipped to the inside of the sun visor.

The last two items were designed to hold packs of cigarettes and books of matches and, because my father did smoke, I'm sure they were useful gifts.

If I had had more money, I might have bought him the Prest-A-Lite—which was advertised as a "luxury accessory." This device could be clamped to the steering column of any car. It held over a pack of cigarettes and dispensed them with ease.

When a driver needed a smoke, he pulled down on the device and out popped a cigarette that was already lit!

Ironically, the Prest-A-Lite was advertised on the basis of being safe, as well as more convenient. It required the use of only one hand and it allowed drivers to keep their eyes on the road while lighting up.

"No more pocket hunting for cigarettes and matches," said the promotional copywriters. "And no more daredevil steering, no flame to blow out—no flare to blind you."

Today, with fewer people smoking cigarettes, the market for this accessory would be much smaller and the promotions would be "politically incorrect."

An advertisement for the Prest-A-Lite cigarette dispenser — another auto accessory that has disappeared.

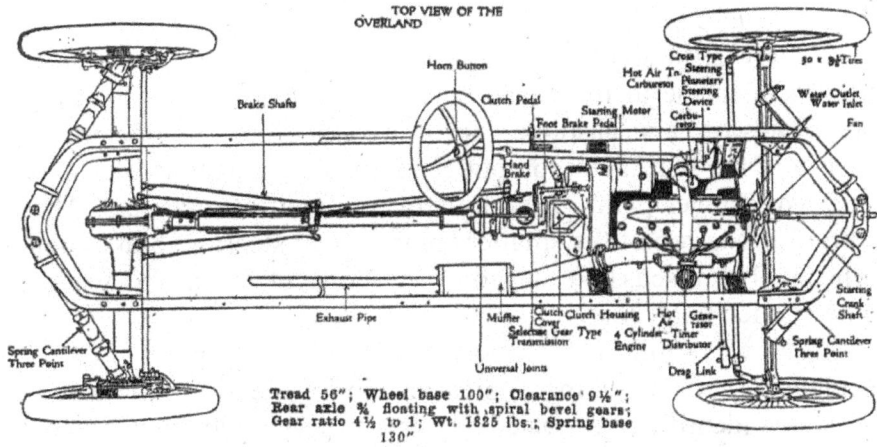

TOP VIEW OF THE
OVERLAND

Tread 56"; Wheel base 100"; Clearance 9½";
Rear axle ¾ floating with spiral bevel gears;
Gear ratio 4½ to 1; Wt. 1825 lbs.; Spring base
130"

Fig. 28. Example of a 4-cylinder car (Overland 4). Note the spring suspension used on this make of car, which is termed "triplex suspension," meaning that there are three points of contact on suspension. Engine, 4 cylinders; bore, 3-⅜"; stroke 4"; actual h. p., 27; crank-shaft main bearing, 3; wheel base, 100"; tread, 56"; rear-axle ratio, 4½ to 1; rear-axle shafts, ¾ floating; transmission sliding gear, three speeds and reverse; clutch, lubricated single-plate type; unit power plant; tire sizes, 30" x 3½"; water capacity, 3¾ gal.; weight, approximately 1825 lbs.; clearance, 9½". See Specifications, pages 1055 to 1062, for later Overland specifications.

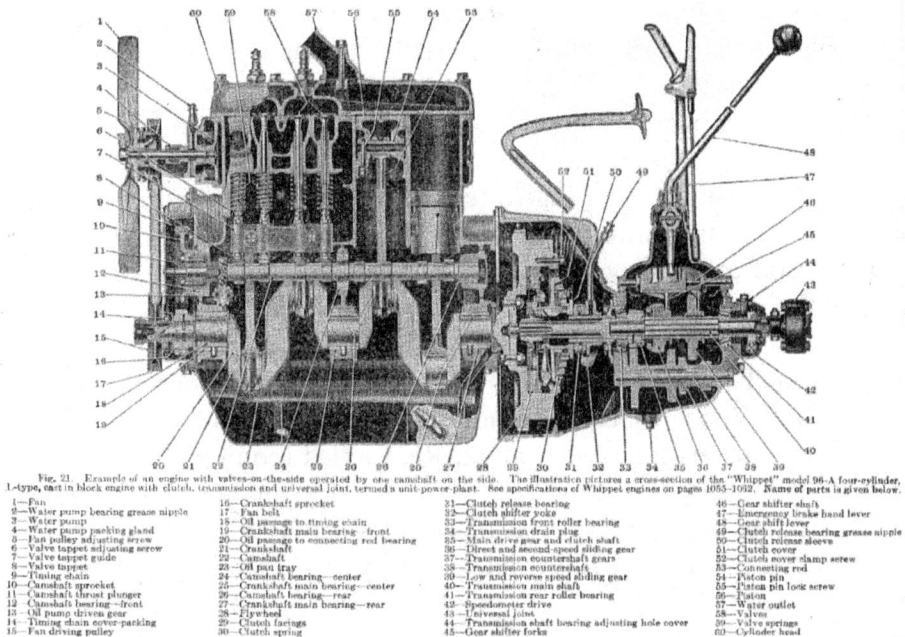

Fig. 21. Example of an engine with valves-on-the-side operated by one camshaft on the side. The illustration pictures a cross-section of the "Whippet" model 96-A four-cylinder, L-type, cast in block engine with clutch, transmission and universal joint, termed a unit-power-plant. See specifications of Whippet engines on pages 1055-1062. Name of parts is given below.

1—Fan
2—Water pump bearing grease nipple
3—Water pump
4—Water pump packing gland
5—Fan pulley adjusting screw
6—Valve tappet adjusting screw
7—Valve tappet guide
8—Valve tappet
9—Timing chain
10—Camshaft sprocket
11—Camshaft thrust plunger
12—Camshaft bearing—front
13—Oil pump driven gear
14—Timing chain cover-packing
15—Fan driving pulley
16—Crankshaft sprocket
17—Fan belt
18—Oil passage to timing chain
19—Crankshaft main bearing—front
20—Oil passage to connecting rod bearing
21—Crankshaft
22—Camshaft
23—Oil pan tray
24—Camshaft bearing—center
25—Crankshaft main bearing—center
26—Camshaft bearing—rear
27—Crankshaft main bearing—rear
28—Flywheel
29—Clutch facings
30—Clutch spring
31—Clutch release bearing
32—Clutch shifter yoke
33—Transmission front roller bearing
34—Transmission drain plug
35—Main drive gear and clutch shaft
36—Direct and second-speed sliding gear
37—Transmission countershaft gears
38—Transmission countershaft
39—Low and reverse speed sliding gear
40—Transmission main shaft
41—Transmission rear roller bearing
42—Speedometer drive
43—Universal joint
44—Transmission shaft bearing adjusting hole cover
45—Gear shifter forks
46—Gear shifter shaft
47—Emergency brake hand lever
48—Gear shift lever
49—Clutch release bearing grease nipple
50—Clutch release sleeve
51—Clutch cover
52—Clutch cover clamp screw
53—Connecting rod
54—Piston pin
55—Piston pin lock screw
56—Piston
57—Water outlet
58—Valve
59—Valve springs
60—Cylinder head

69

A Mechanic's Primer

As a child I visited the library often. When I was thirteen or fourteen, and suddenly interested in cars, I discovered a copy of *Dyke's Automobile and Gas Engine Encyclopedia.*

I knew absolutely nothing about cars, and this book, in simplified form, introduced me to the world of wheels. I learned that there were three different kinds of cars: gasoline, steam, and electric. The opening section of the book told me that the automobile was made up of four component units: running gear, power plant, drive system and control members. There was a fairly brief discussion of the smaller components: steering, brakes, and springs and wheels. The discussion stayed at the concept level, and what I learned could be applied to all cars.

This was followed by a long, fold-out page of automobile nomenclature that taught me something about the basic language of cars. Another page identified the basic body styles, so I could distinguish a roadster from a cabriolet and a sport coupe.

I loved the simplified drawings of a chassis. I had the overwhelming desire to *make* a car, because I was too young to drive, and had no money. Riding my bicycle around the neighborhood, I'd seen an engine lying on the ground, an ancient frame and front end in a field, and some miscellaneous parts beside a garage. I felt no one wanted them, and knew if I could somehow get them home, I could mate the parts into a unified whole. Dyke's book gave me hope, because there were numerous drawings of a stripped chassis with components revealed and identified. It made the concept of a car seem simple.

That's because the first edition of the book was published in 1910, when automobiles *were* simple. It was aimed at the automobile owner who was miles from a garage, or the blacksmith turned mechanic who found himself in the position of trying to repair the new contraption. The fact is, as society made the transition from horse and buggy to automobile, almost no one understood cars. They were a mystery. Dyke's encyclopedia was written to unravel the mystery.

The book said here is an axle, a valve, a magneto—and here is how they function. It simply discussed two basic types of front axles, and their characteristics. Those types were not too different from the axle found on a wagon, so the discussion was limited. Rear axles required more information. The early would-be mechanic who was looking at a Daniels touring that would not move would learn that there were dead axles and live axles, and that there were two types of live axles—plain and floating. Of the latter, there were three types.

The amazing thing about Dyke's encyclopedia is that it presents such a massive amount of information, and that the information is compressed and useful. One section covers gas engine basics. It is followed by a section covering the basic parts of an engine and, in a step-by-step procedure, how to assemble it. The procedure is general and specific, the latter relating to a Whippet flathead four and a Nash 8-80 OHV eight. There's information peculiar to two-cylinder opposed engines, three-cylinder vertical engines, four-cylinder engines with 180-degree cranks, and two-, eight- and 12-cylinder V-type engines.

Cars got more complicated, and subsequent editions included more information. Author A.L. Dyke divided the book into instruction sections. He kept the original material and added sections as new models were built. I found a copy of the 20th edition, published in 1943. Its instruction section number 12 covers the Continental Model 7R Red Seal engine. It's only two pages long, but readers requested information on that engine, as it was used in many cars. Section 13, which covers carburetion, is fifty pages long. It opens with a simple discussion of carburetion principles, then covers the parts of a carburetor and variations found in various early carburetors. Dyke goes on for pages, revealing the workings of carburetors used 50-80 years ago, like Claudel, Franklin, Eagle, Ball & Ball, and even Miller racing models.

The basic book takes you into the era of down-draft carburetors. In 1932, Dyke began adding an addendum to bring readers up to date on things like the Chrysler, Packard, Buick and REO automatic clutch controls, Auburn's two-speed rear, and Plymouth's Floating Power. Addenda No 2—published in 1934—covered things like the new automatic chokes and the new Graham and Franklin superchargers. Dyke also covered general-interest topics, such as streamlining, speed, fuel consumption and the use of engine-testing devices.

By 1943, the book included wiring diagrams, specifications, and the new Chrysler Fluid Drive and GM HydraMatic transmission. There was a lengthy addenda covering the fundamentals of aircraft engines. There were some very odd things, such as a thorough discussion of the taximeters found in cabs. Some sections are shorter, such as those on the British Sunbeam, Rover and Rolls-Royce and a section on overhauling Knight sleeve-valve engines. Other sections, such as those on Model T and Model A Fords, were longer. But it's safe to say that there's something in this volume on most of the era's popular makes.

In addition to practical applications, Dyke's encyclopedia was used as the basis for a home-study course. The publisher made available, for a nominal fee, *Dyke's Self-Starter*, a volume with over 2,300 questions and answers about automobiles. These two books were the equivalent of a trade-school education. For many old-car buffs, much of this information is still relevant. I've seen several copies of Dyke's encyclopedia for sale at swap meets and bookstores. The prices are very reasonable, especially when you consider the incredible amount of information the books contain.

Scooters

In the beginning I simply yearned for mobility; the desire for speed came later.

In the beginning I wanted to move without physical effort, to feel the wind rushing past my face, the ground unreeling below me. The only thing I could compare it to was the feeling of riding my bicycle down an endless hill, without ever having to pedal back up.

Ride a bike and enjoy Chesterfields

They Satisfy

...rs find out the ...ings Chesterfields give them ...nothing else will do

Everything seemed pretty simple to me. I thought that if I were to attach some kind of small gasoline engine to my Western Flyer bicycle I would be mobile. It seemed so easy, in theory. This was about three years after WW II had ended, cars were hard to get because none had been made during the war, and people were riding or driving all kinds of interesting vehicles as daily transportation. I saw guys on Whizzer motor bikes, a Schwinn bike with a small engine, which was exactly what I dreamed of, but I couldn't afford even the bike.

Scooters equipped with compartment for holding small packages have opened a new field for these popular vehicles. Because of low operating costs, they are ideally suited for delivery of small and medium size packages.

Ready for a spin on America's newest means of travel. Large balloon tires tend to increase riding comfort. Simple operation and low operation costs have help to make popular this modern means of transportation.

Then Foster Sporting Goods, a store near my house, became a dealer for Servi-Cycles, and it had a row of about twenty machines out front. The Servi-Cycle was a factory-made heavy-duty bicycle with a gas engine that had a belt drive that turned a hoop within the rear wheel. I couldn't afford one of those either.

Larry Deyoe, a kid I went to school with, got a Doodlebug scooter, which was the smallest of the scooters made back then, just an engine and a seat on a tube framework. He was my age and he rode that Doodlebug all over the neighborhood, without a license, of course. With help from his older brother, he put dual pipes on it using ½" water pipe. It was really just one pipe with another branching out, but I was impressed!

A motor scooter with engine enclosed. Low cost operation has been largely responsible for widespread use of motor scooters. With fuel consumption at a rate making possible 100 or more miles to the gallon, the machines have universal appeal

I began searching newspaper ads for something I could afford. Our paper, *The Oregonian*, had a section called "The Thrifties," which listed items priced under $15, and I read it closely every evening. I hoped to find a Doodlebug, or a little Hiawatha scooter, or a larger Cushman scooter, or a Salisbury scooter, which was deluxe. But I would have happily settled for a homemade affair, a pair of wheels with an old gas washing machine engine. It all seemed so simple to me. I could ride something like that on the sidewalk (never mind that most of the streets in my neighborhood didn't have sidewalks!) and, to be practical, I could use the scooter on my paper route. It seemed so easy: any kind of small engine, a belt or chain to drive the rear wheel—that's all, I wasn't asking for much.

But my father kept telling me that I had to have a driver's license, and license plates, and insurance, and I had to be sixteen to have those. I pouted, I

One of the many motor scooters, showing general construction details. The gas tank is fastened to the frame just ahead of the motor. The starting lever is in a convenient position for left hand use.

was petulant, I threw a fit, but to no avail. I'd heard the stories of motorized whatzits that my father had when he was in grade school, and I'd read that Floyd Clymer had an automobile when he was nine, and a dealership when he was ten! Already I was longing for the good old days!

For persons who wish to take their scooter with them on long trips a special attachment makes it possible to attach them to the rear of the car in the same manner as a trailer.

The Present Refused

It's difficult for a kid to find a gift for an adult. It's partly a matter of money, partly that the years that separate a kid and an adult result in two very different ways of thinking.

When I was 14, I thought I had found the perfect gift for my father for Father's Day: a squirrel knob for his car. In the auto parts store there were hundreds to choose from, and although I can't recall now what that one was like, I was certain it was the perfect gift. But my father gently refused it, saying that it would mar the surface of that great white steering wheel on his 1942 Lincoln Zephyr.

I was probably disappointed, wondering how he could not like it. I thought squirrel knobs were simply beautiful. When I later got my first car I longed to make improvements, but I had no mechanical skills, few tools, and little money. Therefore, the first thing I did was head for that same auto accessory store and carefully select a squirrel knob, because it cost less than a dollar and required only a screw driver to install on the steering wheel.

The knob was gorgeous, I thought, as I stood back to admire my work. It had a chrome plated base and a red plastic top with a dozen stars deep within. It was stamped Hollywood, and although I didn't know whether that referred to the manufacturer or the model that name captured for me the spirit of that knob. It seemed glitzy and racy, somehow sporty, seemingly expensive, like a huge jewel.

More often it appealed to a different audience, guys a few years older than I was, who hunched behind the wheel of an old car, usually a Ford or

Chevrolet, often primered, lowered, with loud duals and oil blow-by coming from under the hood. Collectively, they were called "squirrels," because they raced through the neighborhood and, with the help of that knob, "squirreled" around corners. Hence, the knob was called a "squirrel knob," because it gave the driver a purchase on the wheel and allowed him to spin it around a corner.

It was also called a "necker knob," because it allowed the male driver to steer with one hand while his other arm was around his female passenger.

Some people called it a "suicide knob," perhaps because it could catch on your arm or clothing. When it was offered by the factory, as seen on the 1941 Chevrolet, it was called a "spinner knob." The factory version was built into the wheel, a smaller steering wheel within the wheel, with a bar to grab as you revolved it.

Squirrel knobs were designed with, as Shakespeare said of Cleopatra, "infinite variety." They exploited that modern miracle, plastic. One line had the car's emblem mounted in relief on top. Another had colorful rainbow designs. There were knobs with hand-carved roses floating in clear Lucite, there was the "Moderne" knob, with "concentric alternate circles of white and red, green, blue or black for a third dimensional effect." Then there was the "Sweetheart wheel spinner" which had one of "six lovely girls fetchingly posed and reproduced in natural colors." An added ploy was that the "Lucite lenses enhance lifelike pictures." The lens also magnified the photo of the girl who was, of course, nude.

There were many other designs, with chrome knobs, flowers, funny sayings, animals, you name it. Any auto accessory store had bins of these knobs, hundreds of them.

My question then was: How could anyone not like squirrel knobs? My question today is: Where did they all go?

The Downhill Racers

I want to believe that the desire for mobility is basic, like the need for food, water and oxygen; that it is universal, that every boy yearns for mobility, and that the feeling is especially strong during adolescence. It seems to grow at that awkward age, when a guy is too old to ride his bicycle without feeling like a kid, and yet too young to drive a car.

Or perhaps kids don't have that feeling today, I don't know. This is a much faster world, kids mature more quickly, move into the world more easily. For all I know they might get that same sensation of mobility, even speed, while sitting at a computer. Perhaps to appreciate this story you have to think hard about your own feelings when you were about to graduate from grade school, and what it was that you yearned for.

Or perhaps it's a story about the simple world of 1948, when I was thirteen and yearning for mobility. Everything seemed pretty simple to me: all I needed was a one cylinder gas engine attached to a wheel. It was so fundamental that I began having a recurrent dream, where part of my anatomy merged with a machine; I was being propelled by an engine! I searched the newspaper ads for a motorized scooter, but had no luck.

I had to do something, so my friend, Jimmy Strand, and I built a pair of soap box racers.

I don't know whether that term has any meaning today, and I doubt that any teenager would want to be caught anywhere near a soap box racer in this world of the Internet, but they were popular in the 1930s and 1940s. They were seen in *Our Gang* comics and *Little Rascals* movies. Magazines for boys had articles about them and plans on how to build a soap box racer. Clubs formed, and the goal of most boys was to compete in the national races in Akron, Ohio. Those races were held annually into the 1960s, when—along with Viet Nam, the assassination of the Kennedys and King and wide-spread national unrest—scandal hit the soap box races. A kid's parents put magnets under his racer, which gave him an initial thrust off the line that put him ahead of the other cars! This was illegal, and it became headline news; the world has never been the same.

To appreciate this story you have to think back when you were finishing grade school; you have to think what your life was like, and what it was you were interested in, or obsessed by, and what it was you yearned for. Today everyone seems eager to describe his or her unhappy childhood, usually with an abusive father. Lordy, what they missed.

As I think about my childhood every day seemed an adventure. I loved my B-B gun, my hunting knife, my chemistry set. I rode my bike everywhere and played war in the vacant fields around my house. I read voraciously, books from the library, paperback novels that my father brought home, and comic books. Jimmy Strand and I would lie under the tall Douglas Fir trees in his backyard and read stacks of *Bluebook*, *Argosy* and *True*. The latter was called "The Magazine for Men," a subtitle that would probably cause a furor today. It often had articles by Ralph Stein and Ken Purdy about antique and classic cars. I especially loved Purdy's articles about pre-WW II grand prix racing.

So in that simple world of 1948 the idea of building a soap box racer was downright exciting. The summer of that year was an ideal time to be alive, at least for this thirteen year old kid. I got up early, ate breakfast, then went outside into the brilliant sun and decided what I wanted to do between then and the time I had to go on my paper route. If a day wasn't actually longer back then, it seemed longer, and the summer promised to stretch out forever.

Jimmy and I rode our bikes to Lents and perused the junk stores, second hand stores and Goodwill Store for axles and wheels for our racers. Jimmy bought four spoked wheels, but either I was too broke or too cheap, because I had other plans. Years before my father had built an ingenious contraption for me. It was a board with four wheels and a T-handle; under the board was the drive mechanism. You pushed the handle forward, then pulled it back to get moving, and if you exerted some force you brought the mechanism underneath past an off-set cam that allowed the driving rods to move in an arc. You pushed forward, you pulled back, and if you did this smoothly the machine would move forward. The only problem I saw was that there was no way to steer it, which is no doubt why I didn't use it, as it was, as a soap box racer.

Actually, it was an ingenious machine and my father had put a good deal of work into it. For example, he'd attached a horn from a motorcycle, and it used a long, cylindrical dry-cell battery housed in a thermos bottle. It was a neat rig, and I think I never appreciated it. I took an axe and chopped the steel axles free of their wooden supports and thereby ruined the buckboard. My father was furious, but after expressing his displeasure he walked into the house without punishing me.

Jimmy fixed his wheels and axles onto two by fours, built a platform of light planks and made a body by stretching a white sheet over a minimal wooden framework. My racer, inspired by Purdy's articles about gigantic race cars, was much heavier. I cut the axles in two with a hacksaw, then fixed them to a pair of two by fours with staples. Then I built a platform using a pair of two by eight planks. I built a cowl using two by fours, a flat nose using a huge block of wood and a body using one by eight boards. From the garage I got a name plate that belonged on this heavy machine: Hercules Diesel.

The morning after we finished our racers we were ready to tackle the hill. My mother fixed a lunch and a jar of water to take along, and I threw a hammer and a bag of nails inside the racer. I had no idea how heavy the racer was until I began pulling it to Jimmy's house. I felt like a Chinese coolie, or a slave working on the great pyramids in ancient Egypt, pulling that heavy machine by its steering ropes over the unpaved, bumpy trails that passed for roads in parts of my neighborhood. It must've been a strange sight to the housewife who looked out her window, and I'm certain that no teenager today, used to a light, fast skateboard, would be caught dead pulling that contraption.

I met Jimmy at his house and we set out, pulling our racers over to Foster Road, and along Foster to 112th Street, where we looked up the steep road to the top, far above. Recently I drove down that same hill. Of course almost everything has changed; there are hundreds of houses where in 1948 there were fields of impenetrable blackberry bushes and forests of fir, and now there's a steady stream of traffic where in the old days we might not see a car during an entire day. The only thing unchanged is the hill, which descends Mt. Scott for perhaps a mile, and is so steep I'm amazed that we had the guts to scoot down it in our racers.

But first we had to drag our racers up it, no easy task, and then decide how high we wanted to go. By the time we got halfway up and looked back down we decided that we'd gone far enough. We flopped on the ground beside the road, sweating, and I drank from the Mason jar. I unwrapped the wax paper and ate half a peanut butter sandwich. Jimmy and I joked about crazy things that probably only the two of us found funny.

It was so peaceful on the hill. Grasshoppers clacked in the tall grass, and Oregon Grape seeds popped open in the hot sun. Below, Portland unfolded, its limits clearly marked by forests and lower vegetation. In the calm, I could hear my heart beat. It seemed as if we could stay on the mountain, forever young.

But then it was time. I pulled on a pair of my father's old motorcycle goggles, got the soap box racer in the middle of the road and waited. I thought about everything, and then decided; I pushed away with my feet. The racer moved slowly for about twenty feet, and then began to pick up speed. I held the steering rope tightly in both hands, and as the racer moved faster I was barely able to keep it straight. The vibrations were terrible. For a brake I had nailed an upright two by four to the frame beside me; the idea was that I could pull on the brake and the two by four would drag on the pavement to stop the car. I was zooming downhill, and although I wanted to apply the brake I was unable to let go of the rope; I could not steer it with one hand. Because of the severe vibrations, the two by four brake handle slowly descended, touched the pavement and went flying high into the air.

Now I had no brake, the rope steering was very imprecise and I began drifting slowly to the right, toward the only obstacle in sight, a huge oak tree. But before I got near it the left rear wheel simply collapsed and although the axle dragging on the road must have slowed me somewhat, the racer continued to head to the right. Momentum sent the car ahead, and when I think of that moment I imagine lines of speed coming from the car and myself, like a comic book drawing. I was moving downhill, at speed, through the heat of day, toward a single oak tree which rose like a skyscraper.

Then I was off the road. As I recall, there was a length of black tile pipe beside the road, perhaps water pipe left from some project, and I hit that at an angle and the racer flipped over, bounced high in the air, dumped me out and perhaps turned a couple times before crashing to earth. Face down in the tall grass, I lay motionless, curious whether my arms and legs worked, and because I felt almost no pain I grinned: it was the perfect wreck! Even before I raised my head and looked around I was reliving the accident, and in my mind the car hit harder, bounced higher, turned over in the air, then again and again.

I got up, stood, bruised but unbroken. I waved to Jimmy, who was a distant figure midway on the hill. The left rear wheel of the racer was a twisted mess, and after one run my racing was over for the day. But I was ecstatic, the speed trial was a huge success, better than I could have imagined.

Jimmy shouted, began to descend, the small car picking up speed, the white sheet body fluttering. He went past at a fast clip, clear to the bottom and around the curve, out of sight. When he dragged his racer back we discussed our runs in detail, noting every nuance and I relived my wild run repeatedly. What others might have seen as failure I saw as sheer delight: for a long minute I had felt the rush of wind, and had known the joy not just of mobility, but of speed.

A *True* Story

Before the advent of mass-market automotive magazines—*Speed Age* and *Road & Track* in 1947, *Hot Rod Magazine* in 1948, *Motor Trend* in 1949—there was really only one publication that featured articles about interesting automobiles, and that was *True*. Unlike its competitors, such as *Esquire* and *Argosy*, *True* did not use fiction; it published only non-fiction, or "true" writings.

Sub-titled "The Man's Magazine", *True* informed its readers about things which, from its start in 1936 and through the next three decades, were considered "male subjects". There were articles about hunting, fishing, camping, travel, guns, men's fashions, books, tobacco, liquor, boxing, bullfighting, the old west, Petty and Vargas girls, etc. Much of that is now considered "politically incorrect", but it was a very different world in those days, when men and women seemed to be interested in separate subjects. A subscription to *True* was like having membership in a fraternal lodge, where a guy could sit in a comfortable chair before the fireplace, smoke his pipe, maybe have a toddy and, at least for an evening, vicariously travel the world or go back in time. The magazine had a huge appeal, with a circulation of two million by the mid-1950s.

A subject that interested most men was automobiles; *True* published articles on new cars, antique cars, auto racing, highway safety and related automotive topics. It often used articles on historical auto racing, in Europe and America, during the first three decades of the century. In 1950 that was almost recent history, but information about the big racing Benzs, the Chitty-Chitty-Bang-Bang machines and cars like the huge, square Fiats was scarce. It was certainly all new to me, and I took the information to heart; it influenced my first soap box racer, which was big and square, overbuilt, and so heavy I could barely pull it to the top of the hill!

The person behind the decision to include automotive material was Ken Purdy, possible the first interesting, knowledgeable and literate American automotive writer. (When he left *True* he became fiction editor for a new magazine, *Playboy*.) He was *True*'s sixth editor, and the first to see a need for automotive material to balance out the magazine's content. A skillful editor and writer, Purdy was able to attract other automotive writers and artists, such as Tom McCahill, who made a career of road testing cars, and Peter Helck, who painted several racing scenes that became *True* covers. Helck was also an enthusiast, author of *The Checkered Flag*, and owner of Old Number 16, the famous 1906 Locomobile that was the first American car to win the Vanderbilt Cup race in 1908.

Ken Purdy wrote numerous articles about cars and drivers. A wonderful example, written from the heart, is the article/obituary on Tazio Nuvolari, which Purdy gave, *gratis*, to *True* for inclusion in the 1953 automotive yearbook. He was also the author of several respected books, including *Motorcars of the Golden Past*, *Wonderful World of Automobiles* and *Kings of the Road*. Stirling Moss's *All But My Life* was written "face to face" with Ken Purdy.

He was also an enthusiast, and the owner of a 1913 Mercer Raceabout, once raced by Barney Oldfield, which Purdy bought in the late 1940s, restored and wrote about in an article, "The Mighty Mercer". Purdy drove that antique extensively, as he later drove his Type 37 Bugatti. Writing and wrenching were integrated activities. Editing a magazine did not happen in a void; articles about cars appeared in *True* because Purdy loved cars. In 1974, after Purdy's death, Swann Galleries held a public auction of his automotive books and memorabilia. His library was extensive and included automotive books and magazines, annotated galley proofs, signed artwork and photographs, Purdy's own Bell Toptex racing helmet in a carry case and his gray driving suit, which the catalog describes as "worn".

1951 Daytona Beach Trials, *or* How Fast Was That Nash?

When I was in grade and high school, and for a time after, I took one bath a week. It seems unlikely now, but I'm sure that was true. My parents grew up at a time when bath water had to be heated in copper boilers and buckets on a wood stove, and that was the case in our house until I was about six, when we got a gas kitchen range. When a fire had to be built and water heated, a bath was a big deal; it was usually done once a week, winter or summer, and it became a Saturday night ritual. Even when one only had to turn on a faucet to get hot water, bathing was limited.

The notion that I took only one bath a week comes as a revelation; it's something I haven't thought about for decades. Our house, like most built early in the century, lacked a shower, and all this stuff about bathing came about when I was reminded of my first showers, in high school gym class. During freshman and sophomore years, everyone had to take PE. We were told we needed the exercise, but I now suspect that the real reason was to get everybody in the shower two or three times a week.

I hated PE. I hated it before class even started, when I had to go to the department store with my mother and buy a jock strap! Then I had to wear it, along with a T-shirt, dorky tan shorts and cheap black tennis shoes. The outfit was stupid looking, and designed, I thought, to emphasize our skinny arms and legs. It was a degrading experience. The coaches didn't dress that way; they wore sweat pants and jacket.

But the greatest indignity was when, at the end of class, we had to shed those clothes and take a shower. I tried various ways to avoid it but I'd get caught. So there I was, naked, with fifty other naked kids I barely knew, hanging on to my soap and towel, trying to hide myself while slipping into a shower without making human contact, quickly getting wet and then running, barefoot, over the slippery cement floor, back to my locker.

The only hint of pleasure during that ordeal was that there was time to talk. Everyone was jabbering, perhaps from honest enthusiasm, perhaps as compensation so we'd forget we were naked. The discussions covered sports, social clubs, clothes and, of course, girls, but I seem to remember the ones around me that had to with cars. None of us was old enough to drive, and most of us knew little about cars, but we had opinions! One guy was certain that a new Olds 98 was faster than a new Olds 88 because the former had a bigger number. One kid was certain that a V-8 engine would never fit in a Model A Ford, while another kid, a Chevy enthusiast, claimed to know that Chevrolet would soon do away with its traditional in-line six cylinder engine and come out with a V-6!

Most kids were loyal to the make of car driven by their father. There were Ford fanatics, the Chevy bunch, and those who swore by MoPar products. Then there were the oddballs, a guy who kept talking about Hudson, or Nash, or Studebaker or Packard. In high school kids are quick to judge their fellow students, and often eager to ostracize. The sheer number of Ford and Chevy fans could silence the lone kid who believed in, say, Packards.

But some interesting things were quickly happening. Hudson brought out "Twin-H Power," a dual carburetor set-up for its in-line engine, while Oldsmobile and Cadillac came out with the new OHV engines in 1949. Then in 1951 Chrysler brought out a new 180 hp V-8, and that was a topic of conversation after many showers. We had no idea what a "hemispherical combustion chamber" might be, but we could figure out numbers and we knew that 180 hp was a lot. In the context of Chrysler, no one mentioned his father's Kaiser or Frazer!

It's difficult today to remember how fast some of those cars of the early `Fifties were, or whether that oddball Nash enthusiast's arguments had any merit. But we can get an inkling by citing the record. By 1951 the horsepower race had heated up considerably, and, like the kids in my gym class, almost everyone was interested in the top-end speed of the new cars. During the week of February 4th, 1951, the National Association for Stock Car Racing (NASCAR) held straightaway timed runs at Daytona Beach, Florida, to see how well the various new models performed.

In the 1950 trials the fastest speed was set by Joe Littlejohn in a 1950 Oldsmobile 88 that turned 100.28 mph. The big question was: would that record be broken, by which car and by how much? Everyone, of course, was wondering how fast the new 180 hp Chrysler V-8 would go.

The timed runs were held on the beach over a measured mile. The course was described as "excellent" with "cement-like sands" so slippage was extremely limited at speeds up to 150 mph. The cars were strictly stock, taken directly from the assembly line, driven a few hundred miles to break in the engines and taken to Daytona. Because these were stock models, the kind of car the man on the street could buy, and because speed did sell cars in those days, it was believed high speeds at Daytona would mean high sales.

A 1951 Hudson Hornet driven by Marshal Teague won the 160-mile Grand National Circuit Race held on the circle track; the factory stock model had an average speed of 82.39 mph. A stock Hudson Hornet was a terror on the track back then, but, oddly, Hudson did not finish in the straightaway speed trials. The NASCAR trials, headed by Bill France and Cannon Ball Baker, attracted 13 makes of cars from 16 states; the cars were entered by owner-sponsored teams and not by the factories. The makes, all strictly stock, included Nash, Hudson, Chrysler, Cadillac, Kaiser, Lincoln, Ford, Studebaker, Buick, Oldsmobile, and Plymouth. Also present was a Nash Rambler and a couple of foreign makes, MG and Riley.

The practice runs were held on February 6th; but the speeds were unofficial. The fastest car was a 1950 Lincoln that was driven by Tim Flock; it turned a two-way average of 103.96 mph. Nash took fifth and sixth places, driven by noted racers; Johnny Mantz's 1951 Nash Ambassador turned 96.17 mph, and Curtis Turner's 1951 Ambassador turned 92.41 mph.

Those were unofficial times because some cars were competing with the exhaust disconnected. The February 7th trials were postponed until the 8th because of bad weather. Tim Flock, in a 1950 Lincoln, turned the fastest official time, with a two-way average of 102.07 mph. However, officials discovered that the exhaust pipe was so loose that when they plugged the tailpipe the engine operated smoothly, so they put his car in a modified class, where he took first place. Mundy's 1950 Cadillac turned 99.34 mph, three mph slower with the exhaust pipe attached. That left Tom McCahill as the top dog; his `51 Chrysler turned 100.13 mph.

And what of Nash? Johnny Mantz's 1951 Nash turned the fifth fastest time, with a two way average of 94.29 mph. He was slightly slower than a 1949 Cadillac and a 1950 Lincoln, and ahead of several new Oldsmobiles.

Curtis Turner's 1951 Nash Ambassador turned an average of 92.17 mph, which was good for 10th place. Two other 1951 Nashes came in 12th and 14th, with speeds of 90.55 mph and 89.45 mph, respectively. Curtis Turner also drove a little Nash Rambler to a top speed of 77.57 mph.

A contemporary article in *Motorsport* noted: "Nash sent two stalwarts (from engineering), Earl Monson and Jim Moore, to watch the boys run. Nash was further represented by Chad Lawlor, advertising and sales director, and Bill Haworth, drum beater." Of the 13 makes of cars competing, Nash was singled out in the text to show that the Nash factory was interested in the stock class Daytona speed trials.

POWER and SPEED

WORLD'S MOST FAMOUS MOTOR BOOK!

120 PAGES! 200 ILLUSTRATIONS!

Racing Automobiles, Motorcycles, Airplanes described. Nothing like this unusual British Book to thrill and instruct those interested in HIGH SPEED EQUIPMENT. ILLUSTRATED descriptions of the WORLD'S greatest speed events.

Articles by WORLD FAMOUS SPEED KINGS . . . Captain Geo. Eyston . . . John Cobb . . . Sir Malcolm Campbell. John Cobb writes his story of SPEED at Bonneville Salt Flats, with closeup photos of car, driver, designer. Complete details of runs and times. Descriptions of Campbell's Bluebird . . . Eyston's THUNDERBOLT.

Bonneville and WORLD'S STRAIGHT-AWAY RECORD CHART. Descriptions of cams, compression, valves, superchargers, valves, famous speed engines. International race teams, drivers and cars shown include British, French, Italian, German Auto-Union. Brooklands speed tuning data.

MOTORCYCLE SECTION includes photos, description of famous Isle of Man T.T. Road Race by Graham Walker, Editor English magazine, "Motorcycling." Postpaid $2.50

THE MODERN STEAM CAR and Its Background

100 PAGES — By Thomas S. Derr — 51 ILLUSTRATIONS

An interesting, practical book on steam cars. Written by one of America's outstanding Steam Engineers. Steam history from the start . . . all about early steamers and the "magic of steam" — U. S. and foreign units described. An article by Mr. Stanley included as a section of the book . . . Engines, boilers, generators, valves, etc. . . . How to drive and care for a steam car. An unusual and informative book. Postpaid $2.00

Floyd Clymer's HISTORICAL MOTOR SCRAPBOOK!

Interesting • Educational • Historical
Humorous • Ancient Motor History

These Scrapbooks consist of ads, specifications, descriptions of large numbers of early day Automobiles and Motorcycles. Included in each is an article by Floyd Clymer describing his early connection with cars and motorcycles. A section is devoted to the history of many makes of the past . . . the men that made them . . . and the companies that flourished in by gone days.

FIRST EDITION — 136 Pages. Over 200 makes illustrated, described, includes "Chevrolet V-8," Friction Drive Plymouth, Ford "T" and "S," Overland . . . [illegible] Elmore, Lincoln [illegible], Studebaker Electric, Ford-Selden patent suit details, [illegible] Adams, Olds, Reo, Knox, Orient, Pope, Sears, Maytag, Maxwell, Hupp, Buick, E-M-F "30," Rambler, Cadillac, Autocar, Flanders, Lambert, Moon, Stanley, White, foreign cars, others. MOTORCYCLE SECTION INCLUDES . . . Pierce 4, Thomas, Yale, Pope, R-S, Indian, Harley, Ace, Cleveland, Merkel, N.S.U., M-M, New Era, Dayton. Steam and front wheel drive motorcycles. No. SB-1 POSTPAID $1.50

SCRAPBOOK No. 2—A continuation of the story by Floyd Clymer. 224 pages . . . An entirely different group of cars and motorcycles illustrated and described . . . 2-cycle Olds, air-cooled Chevrolet, Buick 2-cylinder, Studebaker 2-cylinder, Carter twin-engine car, Deere, Corbin, Multiplex, Locomobile, Pierce, Glide, Northern, Franklin, Case, Cole, King, Dorr, Dodge, Brickenbacker, Stutz, 200 others. Motorcycle section . . . Does not replace No. 1 Scrapbook . . . it's entirely new and different. No. SC-2 Postpaid $1.50

100% STEAM CAR EDITION OF SCRAPBOOK — Nothing but Steamers. Over 40 makes listed. Many illustrated, described with ads, photos, specifications. Stanley, Doble, White, Ross, Grout, Skene, American, Locomobile, Mobile, dozens others. Steam race cars . . . see Marriott in world's record-breaking Stanley . . . Webb Jay in White "Whistling Billy." Complete "Questions and Answers" section on Stanley . . . 50-page history steam cars included in book. All about mechanism, boilers, generators, condensers, engines, controls, valves, burners, chassis. The interest in steam cars is at high pitch now . . . get this book. Most complete data on steamers ever published. No. SC-1 Postpaid $2.00

THE WORLD'S WONDER BOOK OF MOTOR HISTORY!

ILLUSTRATED . . . 359 PAGES

AUTHENTIC STORY OF THE AUTOMOBILE INDUSTRY IN AMERICA SINCE ITS INCEPTION . . . By C. B. Glasscock

A most complete book of the growth of early auto manufacturers . . . Ford, Buick, Chrysler, Willys, Dodge, Kettering, Haynes, Winton, Chalmers, Maxwell, The Fisher Bros., Flanders, Duryea, Olds, Durant, Joy, Nash, Cord and other pioneers.

OVER 1600 DIFFERENT U. S. MAKES OF CARS LISTED . . . GAS, ELECTRIC AND STEAMERS.

Historical Photos and Information

MOTOR HISTORY OF AMERICA . . . Postpaid $3.00

A reprint of the FIRST ISSUE 1895

HORSELESS AGE

70 PHOTOS and SKETCHES

This unique and interesting FIRST ISSUE will thrill every lover of early automotive history . . . Read about, and see, GAS, ELECTRIC, STEAM and SPRING driven cars . . . a KEROSENE driven bicycle . . . MOTORCYCLES . . . COMPLETE DETAILS OF AMERICA'S FIRST AUTO RACE . . . FAN DRIVEN BICYCLE . . . EARLY MOTOR SLEIGH . . . MAXIM'S MOTOR TRICYCLE . . . CHARLES DURYEA'S FIRST MOTOR WAGON . . . HAYNES' FIRST CAR . . . UNUSUAL, INTERESTING MOTOR HISTORY IN THE MAKING AND RECORDED FOR THE FIRST TIME IN THIS PIONEER AMERICAN MOTOR JOURNAL.

VOL. I No. 1 — Postpaid $2.00

FOR RACE ENTHUSIASTS

THE SENSATIONAL BOOK OF RACING BY THE LATE SIR MALCOLM OF ENGLAND

176 Pages . . . 41 Photos

This book describes the many speed records made by Campbell and others throughout the speedways of the world . . . and full details of his U. S. trips with famous "Bluebird" at Daytona Beach and Bonneville Salt Flats of Utah.

Read all about the famous drivers and cars of the entire world . . . written by one who knew.

Probably the finest book on automobile racing ever published.

POSTPAID $3.00

SIR MALCOLM CAMPBELL'S BOOK OF FAMOUS MOTORISTS $3.00 — COPYRIGHT 1949 BY FLOYD CLYMER

Paper Bound $2.00

MOTOR WORLD — VOLUME I NO. 2 ISSUE — DECEMBER, 1900

THIS "NEAR FIRST" issue of MOTOR WORLD REPRODUCTION will add an interesting publication to the library of all collectors of HISTORICAL AUTOMOTIVE DATA.

CHOCK FULL of interesting, unusual articles, photos, ads of early day cars . . . MANY ARTICLES ABOUT EARLY MANUFACTURERS and THE EARLY CARS OF AMERICA . . . YOU WILL LAUGH, YET MARVEL at the HISTORICAL data in this VERY early issue reproduction—No. MW-19.

POSTPAID . . . $1.50 A COPY

"THE SALT OF THE EARTH"

THE THRILLING STORY OF

AB JENKINS

World Record Breaker and the

UTAH SALT FLATS

"World's Fastest Speed Course"

Postpaid $1.50

Cloth De Luxe $2.50

The fascinating story of AB JENKINS and the famous MORMON METEOR—illustrated.

A limited number available - ORDER YOUR COPY NOW!

CLYMER MOTORS

Phone FEderal 6410 — 2125 West Pico St. — Los Angeles 6, Calif

The Mile-O-Meter

In 1951, when Mr. Roan, our neighbor across the street, got a nearly-new Ford sedan, he immediately added a Mile-O-Meter gauge. It was an attractive instrument, with a chrome-plated bezel and a five-color face that divided driving conditions into numerous areas. It's hard to believe today, but in 1951 that Mile-O-Meter was a topic of conversation in our neighborhood. In the evening men would gravitate to Mr. Roan's driveway and stand around the Ford, watching that thin needle move as he gunned the engine. I crossed the street with my father and listened as the men discussed the gauge. But I must have gone over several times, because, with great seriousness, I made a large drawing of the instrument's face. It was an awkward drawing, I might add, because it involved concentric circles and numerous segments and lots of small numbers.

The Mile-O-Meter was, of course, simply a vacuum gauge, although that was never mentioned in the advertising. It drew vacuum from the engine, which moved the needle on the gauge. There was no trick involved and the device was useful. When you stepped on the gas, the needle moved to the left, to a red area marked "VERY POOR," with regard to gas usage. And when you let up on the pedal, the needle spun to the right, to the green area marked

"EXCELLENT." The purpose of the gauge was to urge the driver to keep the needle in the narrow area marked "GOOD" for optimum gas mileage.

At the same time, the other circles indicated the "inches of mercury vacuum and motor condition," and the "relative miles per gallon at sea level." Assuming you could drive and study the gauge at the same time, you could learn the "31 Ways Mile-O-Meter helps tune and check (your) motor."

Mile-O-Meter must have been the most advertised auto accessory of all time. In addition to new product promotional spots, there were many partial-page and full-page advertisements for the device. In the December 1951 *Motorsport* magazine, there were six full-page advertisements, including the back cover on both sides. The ads stressed that the gauge was easily mounted, fit any car, could be transferred to a guy's next car, and that it would make the driver proud. "He'll know just how many miles per gallon he's getting at all times, at every speed....He'll save gas and repair bills...he'll know just how efficiently his engine is operating...."

The Mile-O-Meter, manufactured by Gale Hall Engineering, of Boston, Mass., appealed to our desire to own something nice. It was an attractive addition to any dashboard and it was built "with fine watch precision and appearance" and would last a lifetime. It came with a 24-page instruction booklet in a "jewel box" of "Maroon Kifer Leatherette" with the writing embossed in gold. One ad featured the Mile-O-Meter Girl, an attractive, but somewhat sad looking woman in a formal gown, who called it "the gift that keeps giving." She said she had one also, which "instantly tells me when I need service."

The ads cited that, by late 1951, "over one million are in use," which makes me ask where they all went. While I wanted a Mile-O-Meter, I had to settle for a small vacuum gauge that had been on an industrial engine. There was nothing fancy about it, but it did just about what a Mile-O-Meter would do, that is, measure vacuum. After I had mounted it (at a slight angle) atop the '40 Ford dash in my roadster, I drove from my house to Gresham, a small town about 15 miles away, keeping the needle straight up as much as I could. There was so little traffic and so few stoplights that I needed to stop only two or three times. Perhaps, that alone explains the pleasure of driving with a Mile-O-Meter.

It certainly explains how one could drive down the road and stare at a needle moving against a complex background without running into another vehicle.

The Atomic Age

In 1953, one solution to getting rid of old cars was to use them in atomic bomb tests. In one test at the Atomic Energy Proving Grounds near Las Vegas, 100 cars—some new, but most "of ancient vintage"—were blown up.

Donated by major manufacturers and used-car dealers, the vehicles were exposed to the searing heat of a nuclear explosion in order to help assess what might happen to humans trapped in cars in the event of an atomic attack.

Although part of the purpose of that test was to dispose of some old cars, the findings could be useful 60 years later to save some old cars. The tests showed that "a hard top car with the windows open is about as a good a shelter as can be found against the effects of an atom bomb."

With the windows closed, the roof would be forced downward far enough to injure any occupants. But, with the windows open and the occupants crouched on the floor, they would "apparently" be safe anywhere but at ground zero, according to the scientists. "With the windows open, the car afforded protection against shock, heat, radiation and flying debris."

The results of the test created a change in the recommended emergency procedure, which was to leave one's car and seek shelter in a building. One author said, "If we hear the siren blow, we are going to pull over, lie down on the floor and turn on the radio. If we are going to be bombed, we may as well await it in comfort."

The owner of an old car today might use the data from those tests as a justification for keeping the cars. They're not abandoned autos, they're the neighborhood bomb shelters!

THE SUNDAY OREGONIAN, JULY 14, 1946   ***

Shows Today at Your NEIGHBORHOOD THEATRE

AERO 82d-Woodstk. TA 9249
Sunday-Monday
Gale Storm - Raymond Hatton
SUNBONNET SUE
Vera Vague - Robert Benchley
SNAFU

ALADDIN Milwaukie near Powell LA 1492
SUN.-MON. 35¢
Maria Montez - Preston Foster
TANGIER
Allan Lane - Jean Rogers
GAY BLADES

ALBERTA 18th-Alberta MU 3710
Sat. thru Tues.
Edmund Lowe - Brenda Joyce
The Enchanted Forest
in Technicolor
Walt Disney's
PINOCCHIO

AMES 54th-Foster SU 7800
Sun.-Mon.-Tues.
Gale Storm - Phil Regan
SUNBONNET SUE
Richard Crane - Faye Marlowe
JOHNNY COMES FLYING HOME

AVALON S. E. Belmont at 35th
Sat.-Sun.-Mon.
Alice Faye - Dana Andrews
FALLEN ANGEL
Rod Cameron - Fuzzy Knight
Renegade of the Rio Grande

BOB WHITE 65th-Foster SU 2609
Sat.-Sun.-Mon.
Randolph Scott - Ann Dvorak
ABILENE TOWN
Deanna Durbin - Franchot Tone
BECAUSE OF HIM

COLONIAL Albina-Killingsworth GA 0407
SUN.-MON.-TUES.
Maureen O'Hara - John Payne
Sentimental Journey
and Vera Vague in
HISS AND TELL

CREST N. Lmb.-Ptm. UN 1844
Open 1:00 P. M.
SUN.-MON.-TUES.
Ann Sothern - George Murphy
UP GOES

LAURELHURST 28th-Burnside EA 5511
Sat. thru Tues.
Cornel Wilde - Anita Louise
Bandit of Sherwood Forest
—plus—
Penny Singleton - Arthur Lake
LIFE WITH BLONDIE

LINCOLN 3d and Lincoln BE 4292
Sun.-Mon.-Tues.
Dorothy McGuire - George Brent
The Spiral Staircase
—and—
FRONTIER GAL
In Technicolor

LOMBARD Lmbd.-Albina MU 0292
Sun.-Mon.-Tues.
George Brent - Dorothy McGuire
THE SPIRAL STAIRCASE
—plus—
Ida Lupino - Sydney Greenstreet
Pillow to Post

MORELAND SE Mil. Bybee LA 5257
Sat. thru Tues.
Bing Crosby - Ingrid Bergman
THE BELLS OF ST. MARY'S
News—Walt Disney Cartoon

MT. TABOR S. E. 49-Haw. LA 1702
Sun.-Mon.-Tues.
Fredric March - Alexis Smith
ADVENTURES OF MARK TWAIN
—plus—
Osa Massen - Byron Barr
TOKYO ROSE

MULTNOMAH Multnomah, Or. CH 8696
Sun.-Mon.-Tues.
Clark Gable - Loretta Young
CALL OF THE WILD
—and—
Eddie Dean - Jean Barton
ROMANCE OF THE WEST

OREGON S.E. Div.-35th VE 9683
Sun.-Mon.-Tues.
Academy Award Winner
Ray Milland
THE LOST WEEK END
—plus—
Frances Langford - Alan Carney
RADIO STARS ON PARADE

PLAZA Hawth.-20th EA 1707
Sat. thru Tues.
Cornel Wilde - Anita Louise
The Bandit of

93

Spring Cleaning

Between Easter and Father's Day there is an awakening of color: iris, daffodils and gladiolus, Easter eggs, Hawaiian shirts. The grime of winter is scrubbed from the family car, and it's waxed until the paint seems new. The resurrection takes place. There is the question of what to give the father on his day, and it's usually something for that awakened car.

Perhaps a chrome-plated outside rear view mirror that simply clamps to the door; better yet, a pair of them. Less practical, but more fun, would be a steering wheel knob for the quick turns; it's often called a "suicide knob," but this model, we're assured, "can't catch on a sleeve"!

For the father who is a cautious driver, with his feet on the floor, how about a pair of waffle mats? Both colorful and practical are the "fences" that attach to the dashboard via suction cups or magnets; they hold necessary things such as cigarettes, matches and old parking tickets.

Even though older cars came from the factory with wing windows, the "draft eze" wind deflector was a popular item; it kept the wind away from the occupants' face and, like the fences it came in all colors, adding a gay touch to what might be a drab car.

A bug deflector, in a matching color, was available to clip to the hood ornament. Or that spot might be reserved for a huge winged hood ornament, chrome plated, if the entire family kicked in some loot.

Not for every driver was the "Lindberg Propeller," but the mature father with latent visions of speed wanted one. It sat at the front of the hood, and when the car was in motion that seven-inch propeller would "spin freely on [a] roller bearing"; that sporty touch would start conversations, give you a sense of adventure and pull you into summer.

The Fisher Body Craftsman Guild Competition

From 1930 until 1968, the General Motors Craftsman Guild held an annual model car contest for boys between the ages of 12 and 18. The purpose of the contest was simple: to inspire an interest in automotive design, and to discover early on talented youngsters who might want to make a career of working in the field, especially for General Motors. Because the contest was sponsored by a major corporation, and because the prize money was significant, the yearly event loomed large in the minds of youngsters who were crazy about cars and especially those whose families lacked the money to send them to college. Thousands of boys entered the competition over the years, and thousands more, like myself, intended to enter but somehow never completed the model.

One fellow who did enter was Gale Morris of Portland, Oregon. In 1948, when he was 13, he worked Saturdays at Vic's Hobby Supply, and because he had been building model cars for years the owners, Vic and Connie, urged him to send in his application. In addition to the entry forms, Morris received an instruction manual. This was not a simple sheet of instructions, but a small magazine with rigid rules.

All models had to be a "five or six passenger sedan," no more than 16 ¾ inches long, between six and 6 ½ inches wide, at least five inches high, with restrictions on front and rear tread measurements, wheel size, bumpers, luggage space, front and rear overhang, road clearance, passenger space, etc. The builder had to indicate the door and window outlines, door handles, illuminated rear license plate and grilles or other openings for cooling. The model could be made of wood, plaster "or other substantial material or combination of materials," but not clay. The body had to be solid, without an interior or engine; the doors, hood and trunk could not open, and the wheels could not turn. Also, "no part or detail is required to…operate."

The instructions alone weeded out boys who were given to flights of fancy, whose dreams would not translate into what the Guild deemed a practical model. Moreover, if a boy could follow the instructions to the letter it said something about his ability to read, comprehend, and work with committees and indirectly it said something about his character. In fact, the instructions about building the box in which the model was shipped were so detailed I suggested that perhaps the judges made their decisions based on the workmanship put into the box!

When Gale Morris entered the contest in 1948 the auto industry was in transition, moving from prewar body styles to the envelope body style. Morris, in a written statement that accompanied the model, set up the criteria for his design. It would have a V-8 engine, a girder box-type frame, and torsion bar suspension. The roof would be braced with a heavy girder in the middle and side braces that went down to the corners. The hood and trunk would be operated via a hydraulic lifter mechanism activated from inside; the doors would be opened by push buttons that allowed the doors to spring out two inches, with a safety latch. There would be grilles for ventilation; the bumpers would be mounted on spring shock absorbers, and the tail and parking lights would be mounted in rubber and built into the bumper. Many of these were advanced ideas, with an emphasis on styling and safety; some related to the newly-introduced Tucker, and some would find acceptance on American production cars several years later.

A standard guide and kit were available from the Craftsman Guild, with ready-made wheels and other parts, but Morris didn't use them. He carved the body from balsa wood and turned his own wheels on a lathe using maple. The front and rear bumpers were carved from balsa wood and painted silver. Morris made all the chrome trim using lead solder. But before adding the bumpers and trim it was time to give the finished car a color coat.

HOW TO BUILD A MODEL CAR

FISHER BODY
CRAFTSMAN'S GUILD

Regarding paint, the instruction manual said only, "Paint model according to your own ideas," but it was obvious that paint was extremely important. Morris used a heavy metallic green lacquer, which had to be sprayed on. Aerosol spray cans weren't available in 1948, so Morris made his own spray outfit using a hand pump and an air tank to avoid pulsations. This was pretty ingenious thinking for a 13 year old boy, and it paid off. The paint was beautiful.

Later, when Morris saw the other boys' models, he noticed that most of them had used a non-metallic paint, applied with a brush, sanded down and rubbed-out to get a smooth finish. He remembers that several cars had metallic paint jobs, but when he asked the builders how they'd applied the paint their answers were vague. Perhaps someone had helped them.

When the car was finished, Morris built a shipping box according to the Guild's directions. It had to be made of plywood, braced at the corners, with flathead wood screws three inches apart on all sides. At the bottom he placed a wooden block with two large pegs sticking up; these pegs fit into two holes in the bottom of the model. The car was placed inside the box, with padding on all sides, and the top screwed on. He filled out the mailing label and took it to the post office.

There was an interminable wait, and in the spring of 1949 Morris got a telegram congratulating him on having won both the junior state award and the regional award. The state award was $150.00 cash, a lofty sum for a young boy in those days, and the regional award meant that he would get an all-expense trip to Detroit for a week. He and his parents were ecstatic; this award would change his life, but he wouldn't know until later whether he had won a scholarship. The scholarship winners would be announced in Detroit.

Morris was asked to write a 500-word autobiography, and to send it, along with a photo of himself ("we'd prefer a portrait, but a snapshot will do") and his ring size as determined by a jeweler, airmail special delivery to the Guild. This was a high-buck, impressive contest, run with class.

Not only did Morris receive a beautiful Guild ring, but his parents were sent money to buy him a sport coat, slacks, dress shirt and necktie. The Guild wanted the boys dressed up for the Detroit events, and it neither assumed that every boy had such an outfit nor that all parents had the money to buy such clothes for their son. The Guild also sent Morris spending money for the trip, the Guild ring and lifetime membership in the Guild, which included a wooden lapel pin and a newsletter that came out for years.

He was asked to sign the Guild pledge card: "As a member of the Fisher Body Craftsman Guild, I pledge myself to build honestly with my own hands all the work I may undertake in the Guild...to perfect myself in workmanship and designing, to conduct myself in all things in the industry with steadfastness and fair dealing befitting a natural craftsman."

That August Morris said goodbye to his parents and got on the train; it went first to Seattle, where he met another regional winner, then on to

Chicago, where they met the other boys from all over the United States who were competing for scholarships.

Three train cars were reserved for the boys, and they traveled together to Detroit. The week in Detroit was jammed with activities. A police escort met the train, and guided the boys' busses to the Statler Hotel, where they stayed. There were 21 senior winners and 22 junior winners (one duplicate award); the difference had to do with the winner's age. They saw the city, visited the General Motors Proving Grounds, toured the Cadillac plant, and were feted at the plush Bloomfield Hills Country Club. There was even a boat trip to Canada, and although the distance was short it was an international experience for the boys, most of whom had not traveled far from home up to that time.

On August 24, 1949, there was a huge banquet at the Statler, where the scholarship winners would be announced. This event was a big deal. It was broadcast on national radio, and Morris' parents were listening in Portland.

The master of ceremonies was Bob Considine, a popular sportscaster. There were more than 300 people at the banquet, and they represented a who's who of the automotive world, starting with L.C. Goad, the president of General Motors, Edward Cole of Cadillac, and Charles Kettering. Previous winners at the alumni table included Virgil Exner.

The collected body sang the Guild song, were welcomed, then had a deluxe several-course meal. Finally it was time to announce the winners of the Guild scholarships, and Morris was thrilled to hear his name called. He won third place in the national competition, which meant he would receive $2,000 for his education, a considerable sum in those days. His parents sent him a telegram of congratulations.

On Friday it was time to leave, and the group boarded the S.S. North American for a leisurely trip to Chicago, with a stopover at Mackinac Island. Morris left with only a slight sense of regret. By now he realized that most of the boys who were there had entered previous Guild contests. Once you won a scholarship you couldn't enter the contest again, and Morris felt that if he had not won that year he could've entered the following year and he might have won a senior award, which was $3,000.

But they could not have given a scholarship to a more deserving craftsman. In his autobiography he said he was "not certain what his final occupation will be but he's interested in mechanics and car designing."

First, of course, he had to attend high school, and the prize money was put into a trust until he was 18. In the interim, he built several hot rods, including a pair of channeled, full-fendered 1932 Ford pickups and a 1939 Mercury convertible. The Mercury was built twice, with the final version resembling a Mercedes Benz 300 SL coupe.

After high school, Morris studied at the Los Angeles Design Center, using the money he had won in the GM contest, and graduated with a degree in industrial design. Rather than design cars, however, in 1958 he took a job with Techtronics, Co., located in Portland, Oregon, and became the company's first industrial designer. He recently retired after 40 years with the company.

A few years ago the Smithsonian Institute became interested in collecting outstanding models from the GM competition "as a record of the influence that these young designers have had upon the history and evolution of the American automobile industry." Morris's model was identified as an outstanding example of the late 1940s contest winners; he was asked to make a gift of his model to the permanent collection of the National Museum of American History.

Morris had kept his model for nearly 50 years and while he was reluctant to part with it he also felt honored that it had been selected. He agreed to send the model, but first he had to build a special box in which to ship it, a task that seemed as difficult as building the original box had been.

NATIONAL AWARD WINNERS

First Senior Award, $4,000 Scholarship

Fourth Senior Award, $1,000 Scholarship

• • •

FISHER BODY CRAFTSMAN'S GUILD
Sponsored by Fisher Body Division of General Motors
Detroit 2, Michigan

Zern's Zany Nash

One of the more successful automobile advertising campaigns in print was the Ed Zern ads for Nash that appeared in *True* magazine at mid-century. The ads first appeared in 1949 issues of the magazine, and continued into the 1950s, so the factory, the ad agency and the readers must have found them effective as well as amusing.

True was subtitled *The Man's Magazine* at a time when people did not worry if something was gender offensive or politically correct. It featured articles and advertising concerned with men's fashions, pipe tobacco and cigars, liquors, firearms, cartridges, camping, fishing and hunting. Many considered it to be more "manly" than *Esquire*, and *True* published only "true" pieces, unlike *Argosy*, the other magazine competing for the same market.

It was the outdoor sportsman angle that got the Nash ads placed in *True* rather than an automotive magazine. In 1949 Nash cars got a new body, and the ads stressed that the updated Nash had room for all the equipment needed on a hunting or fishing trip. One selling point was the fact that the seats folded into a bed.

Month after month Zern's humorous ads appealed to sportsmen. A typical example is "Man Catches Mermaid," number 26 in the series, found in the April, 1951 issue of *True*. A fisherman fulfills a life-long dream when he "foul-hooks" a mermaid in Florida. He attributes his good fortune to his 1951 Nash Airflyte. The mermaid tells him he "must be off (his) noodle."

To convince her, he cites the car's features. "I've always got the right tackle and equipment with me, including a folding boat and outboard motor, thanks to all the space in that Airflyte luggage compartment! I get exceptional gas mileage so it doesn't cost me much to travel to the hottest fishing spots. And that Airflyte rides so smoothly and handles so easily that I arrive rested, refreshed and fully alert!"

He goes on, mentioning "that wonderful Nash Weather Eye Conditioned Air System, the Twin Bed arrangement, the Airliner Reclining Seat..."

He then suggests that they get better acquainted, but she swims off, goes to a bathhouse, changes into street clothes and drives to her place of employment, the Chamber of Commerce, in her Nash Rambler convertible.

The ads were short, humorous, and covered quickly the features of the new Nash. Even though station wagons were becoming increasingly popular and also appealed to sportsmen, I can't recall any other automobile company advertising in *True*.

Or, if there were other ads, they obviously weren't as memorable as the Ed Zern pieces for Nash.

DUCK-HUNTER DUNKED!!!

No. 24 IN A SERIES OF NASH AIRFLYTE ADS BY ED ZERN

ONCE THERE WAS A DUCK-HUNTER driving through the west in his 1951 Nash Airflyte with Hydra-Matic Drive. When he came to a town way back in the hills where they were holding a Lying Contest, he parked his car and entered the contest.

After the local talent had told about the windstorm that blew the wagon tracks off the hayfield onto the courthouse lawn, and the gopher that burrowed into the side of a dust storm, and the fast-growing vine that wore out the pumpkins dragging them around on the ground, it came the duck-hunter's turn.

"Friends," he said, "I drive a 1951 Nash Airflyte, with Twin Beds and an Airliner Reclining Seat. On account of having coil springs all around, and super-rigid, all-welded Airflyte Construction, it's just about the smoothest-riding car on the market. In fact, one night I was driving through a town at 50 miles an hour and ran over three hogs and the mayor, and never even felt a bump.

"And the next day," the duck-hunter said, "I crawled back into that enormous Airflyte luggage compartment to look for a sack of decoys I had mislaid in there, and got lost. I wandered around in that luggage compartment for three days and three nights, and if I hadn't flushed a covey of quail and shot one with my pistol I'd have starved to death before I found my way out."

The Judges Committee then declared a brief recess, and when it was over the chairman rapped his gavel. "Gents," he said, his voice quivering with rage and indignation, "durin' the recess, me and the boys done some checkin' up. This here stranger left the keys in his Nash Airflyte—so we lined up three hogs and the mayor, and throwed in a deputy sheriff for good measure, and run over 'em at 50 miles an hour.

"Then we opened up the luggage compartment to see how big it really is. And folks, I got somethin' to tell you! *This lop-eared, low-down, no-good, ornery, double-crossin' coyote was tellin' th' TRUTH!*"

So everybody jumped on the duck-hunter and beat him black and blue and took him out and flang him into the horse-trough.

MORAL: *Never leave the keys in your car.*

Nash Motors Division, Nash-Kelvinator Corporation, Detroit, Michigan.

See all three Nash Airflytes for 1951: The Ambassador, the Statesman and the Rambler (in Convertible, Station Wagon and Suburban models.)

"Sell 'N Swap" Magazine Ads

Whenever car lovers get together, sooner or later someone will mention a car they used to own, years ago, and sold; a car they wish they still had today.

That kind of a spark will ignite a conversation that can go on for hours, as others yearn for the car they owned and sold (for a very low price) or the car they almost bought for practically nothing.

Sometimes, the point of the discussion centers on the merits of the car, but usually it has to do with the car's value. Forget that a particular '40 Ford convertible had a couple of dents and burned oil which, back then, made it worth about $300. The ex-owner is still going to talk about what such a car (probably completely restored) is worth today.

It doesn't matter when you first got involved with old cars, they were always cheaper than they are nowadays. In the mid '70s, I was looking for a '32 Ford roadster, and there were a number of such cars—with steel bodies—available in the Midwest, for around $2,000. At that time, I even had the money. Why I didn't buy one of the cars is beyond me. According to *Old Cars Price Guide*, such a car is now worth $18,200 in No. 2 condition and $26,000 in No. 1 shape.

Of course, similar comparisons could be made for just about any old car (except for some that become less desirable and harder to sell). Still, over those 30 years, the majority of older cars have *all* appreciated in value.

This point was brought home to me the other day, as I was paging through a 1953 copy of *Motor Trend* magazine. Toward the back of the old publication was a "Sell 'N' Swap" column with classified ads for cars and parts that were for sale back then.

Now, 55 years ago may seem like a long time for some, but 1953 is recent history for me. I got out of high school that year, and I can remember seeing cars of the '30s being used as daily drivers then.

The Model A Ford that I looked at, as hot rod material, was someone's everyday transportation. The back rows of used car lots had all kinds of ancient vehicles, and they were dirt cheap. A car lot on 82nd Avenue in Portland, Oregon, which was near my house, proudly advertised, "No car over $99!" I'm certain that a Graham, a Packard, or a Lincoln sat on that lot. Who knows—maybe there was even a Cord to buy for less than a $100 bill.

The classified ads in *Motor Trend* were open to any and all types of cars. Back then, however, it made little sense to advertise common cars like a '33 Willys or a '42 DeSoto on a national basis, unless the car was somehow exceptional. Instead, most of the ads featured antiques and classics, with sports cars and a few rods and customs thrown in for good measure.

The variety of cars and parts in the ads is really striking today. Back then, there were no swap meets, so enthusiasts had to search long and hard for obscure cars and parts. However, the vehicles were out there—hiding in barns or garages—or parked under a tree in someone's back yard. You just had to work a little harder to find them.

While there were some serious car collectors at the time, it was more common to run into people who were crazy about a particular make—or a particular car—that they liked for some reason.

Falling under the heading of a serious collector was the advertiser from Missouri who wanted a non-condensing Stanley Steamer. I hope that he contacted another advertiser, from California, who wanted a flow motor and steam gauge for a [model] 10 White Steamer. Both of these men might have also met another California advertiser who wanted a Stanley Steamer and indicated that he would pay $1,000 or more, if the condition of the car warranted it. That was a lot of money to pay for an old car in 1953. Most cars that appeared in *Motor Trend* were advertised for considerably lower prices. Most were easily affordable back then. There was a low-mileage `15 Buick roadster for $900, and a `30 Hupmobile sedan for $175. The Hupp sedan was nearly a throwaway car back then, but somewhat more interesting was the ad for a `25 Franklin sedan, priced at $250.

In case the old-car fans didn't know what they were doing, Robert Gottlieb wrote a column called "Classic Comments" for *Motor Trend*. He was an attorney, and often touched on the topics concerning cars and the law. Gottlieb even had three cars for sale in the issue I was reading, and must have known how to get top buck for them. Two of them—a `31 Auburn and a `32 Auburn—were priced at $75 each!

While I've always admired antique and classics, I've never really wanted to own one. Modified cars have been more interesting to me, personally. So, I would have liked another car that was advertised in *Hot Rod Magazine*'s classified ads, in 1953 or 1954, for $1,500. It was a `39 Ford convertible that was fully customized, and had a `50 Cadillac engine. A friend of mine owned this car from approximately 1975 to 1990. He restored it to its 1953 condition, and sold it to a man in Chicago for around $50,000.

The ads in the old issue of *Hot Rod Magazine* also featured a `49 Mercury convertible with a Chrysler V-8. No price was given and, while I'm certain I could have afforded this car in 1953-`54, I'm not sure I could have given the seller the quick cash he wanted.

The one car that I really wish I had bought from the old ads was described as a two-man race car that won the 1936 Indianapolis 500. It was complete, running, and claimed to be in perfect condition. It was even licensed for the street, and the asking price was $800. The 1936 Indy 500 was won by Louis Meyer, who recently passed away. That win was his third in that race. If the ad was accurate, the $800 car was the old "Ring-Free Special," but its original Miller engine had been replaced.

Looking back over 55 years, we can see that both old cars and land in the suburbs have appreciated in value. If those of us who were reading those classified ads in 1953 could have seen into the future, we would have purchased cheap land, put up a barn or two, and filled them with cheap classic cars. That would have given us a wonderful nest egg for retirement.

Of course, most of us didn't think of old cars as investments back then. They were just something we wanted to play with.

SELL—Four new Dayton wheel rims, size 5 x 16, three new Dayton wheels 4 x 16. $20 each. Four Dayton hubs with new Rudge type wing caps, $20 each. A. Singer, 17066 Smith St., Wyandotte, Mich.

SELL—Two each Cord rear hubs, wing caps, wheels, tires 7.00 x 16 with tubes, $20. A. Singer, 17066 Smith St., Wyandotte, Mich.

SELL OR SWAP—Alfa Romeo, 2.9 liter engine; newly overhauled, new parts, carbs, magneto, blower, clutch and housing. $2250 or take MG. Woestman, 2310 Midlothian, Altadena, Calif.

SELL—V-8 track roadster; full race track engine, gear box and trailer. $275. D. Campbell, 919 Woodster Ave., Akron, Ohio.

SELL—'51 Ford coupe; black, 190 hp '52 Cadillac, overdrive, 3.57:1 rear, engine 175 miles, car 4000, General whitewalls, Continental rear end, radio and heater. $3000. P. Wing, 5531 Washington Blvd., Chicago, Ill.

SELL—New Model T parts; camshafts, bearings, ring gear sets, rear axle bearings, tappets, complete pistons, rods, etc. Also antique speedometers and parts. H. Dissman, 271 E. Dearborn St., Havana, Ill.

SELL—Carbide gas generator running board type, gas light tips, Kero dashboard type light, antique tire gauges, foot feeds, exhaust cutouts, other antique supplies. H. Dissman, 271 E. Dearborn St., Havana, Ill.

WANTED—Stanley Steamer—non condensing; must be complete except for boiler. F. Semple, 11 Danfield Rd., St. Louis 17, Mo.

SWAP—'48 Ford club coupe, Hollywooded, warm engine, all accessories. Trade car and cash for custom conv. Prefer V-8 type engine. G. Phillips, 252 Hwy 99 South, Grants Pass, Ore.

WANTED—Sports car or what have you. State price and condition. If you wish trade, what do you want? C. Hartz, Box 225, Parsons Hall, Terre Haute, Ind.

SELL—'37 Cord trunk back sedan, new paint and upholstery. Engine, transmission and joints recently overhauled at Cord factory. Appearance and performance excellent. $1200. B. Keys, 504 Winters Bank Bldg., Dayton 2, Ohio.

SELL OR SWAP—Excellent steel auto trunk for Packard or Cadillac trunk rack. Want dual manifold for '48 to '52 Packard Eight. F. Van de Water, 822 Ardmore Rd., West Palm Beach, Fla.

SELL—'27 Paige four-door; good body, upholstery and chassis. Original finish and spoke wheels. Easy to restore to top condition. Best offer. H. Roach, 2101 E. Pacific, Spokane, Wn.

SELL OR SWAP—'32 Pierce Eight roadster; sharp, original. Want later V-12 Pierce conv. or '40-'42 Lincoln Continental. C. Wyker, 560 Norton Rd., Columbus 4, Ohio.

SELL—Mark II MG; enthusiast's TD; as new. Am unable to do justice to this superb competition version. Cost as equipped, $2500. Best offer. H. Cuone, c/o Essex County Sanatorium, Verona, N.J. VE 84700.

SWAP—'09 Cadillac touring; mint condition. Want vintage or modern sports car or sell for best offer over my cost of $1800. J. Mattison, 208 E. Wisconsin Ave., Milwaukee 2, Wisc.

SELL—'41 Graham parts; complete engine, transmission, etc.; '37 Dodge 8.5 custom head, dual manifold, carbs, linkage. Best offer. Want five Dayton knock-off wheels, hubs. A. Kabel, 122 S. Spaulding Ave., Chicago 24, Ill.

SELL OR SWAP—'21 Pierce Arrow seven-passenger sedan; new paint, ok to drive. Cost $9000. Make offer or swap for what have you? A. Merrill, Rt. 1, Goffstown, N.H.

SELL—'14 20 hp Stanley steam touring car, excellent mechanical condition. Price $3500 cash, no pictures or offers. H. Wing, Sr., Chapel Rd., Brier, Mass.

WANTED—'18 V-8 Chevrolet, complete to restore. Send photos. W. Morris, 1149 Pecan St., Abilene, Texas.

SWAP—'47 Oldsmobile 8 station wagon, 51,-000 miles, very good condition. $400 balance of contract remaining. For low mileage pre-'40 Cadillac. E. Drone, 911 Webster St., Traverse City, Mich.

SWAP—'49 Buick conv in excellent condition for '41 Lincoln Continental conv. or hardtop with overdrive in top condition. Send complete information. W. Vengen, Box 695, Bluefield, W. Va.

WANTED—XK-120 Jaguar without engine or without engine and transmission. No wrecks. Prefer one on the West Coast. C. Artal, 632 Ellis St., San Francisco, Calif.

WANTED—Copy of "The Insider" published by General Motors in 1911. W. Leland, 4203 Cortland Ave., Detroit 4, Mich.

SELL—'46 Crosley sedan, Willys engine and transmission. Engine needs work. Good for customizing. $125. A. Foster, 421 S. 71 E. Ave., Tulsa, Okla.

WANTED—'48 MG TC; no extras. Advise lowest price and condition. Cash for right car. W. Koontz, Apt. 35 Airbase, Brownsville, Texas.

SELL—'52 Lincoln ohv V-8 engine; dual manifold, chrome accessories. R. Fudge, Jr., 3535 Longridge Ave., Sherman Oaks, Calif.

WANTED—'41 Graham or Skylark Hupmobile chassis and body. Engine means nothing to me. Located in the vicinity of Ohio. Reasonably priced. J. Kuhn, 5252 Broadview Rd., Cleveland 29, Ohio.

WANTED—Used dual manifold for '39 Ford V-8. Also generator bracket and throttle linkage. All replies answered. G. Fitch, 1431 University Ave., New York 52, N.Y. JE 70011.

WANTED—Stutz four-cylinder; any year or model. Send photo if possible. B. Christian, 839 Marsh Rd., Menlo Park, Calif.

SWAP—'36 through '48 Cadillac dual manifold and carb. with air cleaners and linkage for magnetos for '52 Cadillac. P. Wright, Glen Allen, Va.

SELL—'32 Packard 900; mechanically perfect, excellent body and chrome, 50,000 miles, new tires, battery. Photos on request. Best offer over $100. R. De Muri, 10416 S. Calumet, Chicago 28, Ill.

SELL—'27 T touring frame and body, all V-8 running gear, in excellent condition. 5000 miles on new 6.00 x 16 tires. '41 V-8 engine and hydraulic brakes. Good paint, upholstery, sealed beams and '49 radiator. Good road car never raced. Best offer over $750. F. Covert, 5122 N. Gd. River, Lansing, Mich. Ph 55653.

SELL—'33 Auburn speedster; 3.1 rear end, car better than new, quick change wheels. $750. K. Graham, 1935 Myrtle, Kansas City, Missouri.

SELL—'36 Packard V-12 conv.; 84,000 actual miles, $800 worth of engine work done on car in last two years. Write for information. P. Gregoire, 417 South 8th, Pocatello, Idaho.

SELL OR SWAP—MG TC in excellent condition. Never raced, black finish, excellent green leather. Want cash and 500cc Triumph motorcycle, any condition. B. Hansen, 3529 Victory Ave., Racine, Wisc.

SELL—Graham supercharger, $20 or rare '40 Graham club coupe in good shape. Both for $100. J. Woods, 654 Oliver St., N. Tonawanda, N.Y.

SELL—'51 Javelin Jupiter engine with four speed gearbox and radiator, 3800 miles on engine, perfect. $350. H. Towle, Box 62, North Main St., New Hope, Pa.

WANTED—Will pay cash for stock '32 Ford roadster or pay $100 for information leading to purchase of latter. Buffalo, Canada or 250 mile radius. R. Gates, 222 Riley St., Buffalo, N.Y.

SELL OR SWAP—Two diesel electric plants 7½ and 3½ K. W. 110-220 volt AC, perfect condition, for late foreign car. J. Bayer, Rd. 2, Lehighton, Pa.

SELL—Two passenger custom '50 Special Speedster, racing design for highway use. Quality spray beige paint, immaculate appearance, excellent condition, dual outside exhausts. $1000. C. Durso, 29 Franklindale Ave., Wappingers Falls, N.Y.

SELL—'27 T Ford roadster; excellent condition for restoration. Will deliver. $50 FOB. D. Johnson, 781 W. Office St., Harrodsburg, Ky.

SELL—Five quick change Dayton wheels and hubs, $50; double overhead cam Fronty engine, $50; Fronty rocker arm head for T Ford, $15. D. Johnson, 781 W. Office St., Harrodsburg, Ky.

WANTED—Continental spare tire hinge and chrome latch to rear deck. Prefer model for Chevrolet but will consider any make. Send details and prices. W. Stanley, Mead Point, Greenwich, Conn.

SELL OR SWAP—'51 Olds Super 88 four-door with souped engine, Hydra-Matic, safety tubes, whitewalls, all accessories for '51-'52 Pontiac which I can customize. Write for details. Wm. Stanley, Mead Point, Greenwich, Conn.

SELL—'28 Buick Standard roadster; good original condition, needs paint. Many parts for '27 and '28s, '27 touring body, '25 tires, engine. $275. F. Cook, 33 Oakley St., Dorchester, Mass.

Colorful Hues of `50s Not Only On Cars

In 1955 I got a job at Lee Cosart Dodge-Plymouth just as the new models arrived. Although I couldn't afford a new car, it was fun to go to work each day where a "newness" odor permeated everything and I could check out what was in the showroom.

An obvious change was size: the new Dodges and Plymouths were longer than those built during 1953-`54. A second thing that struck me was the seat fabric, which had gold or silver wire running through it. I thought such material, with Naugahyde trim, would be neat in an older car I could afford. I was also struck by three-tone paint jobs. I remembered `40s cars, usually painted a single color, and saw cars of the early `50s, on which the roof was painted a contrasting color, but the use of color on the new models was remarkable.

Critics have commented on the grayness of the Eisenhower-Nixon years, describing the era as "the bland leading the bland." The earlier dominant car colors—black, dark blue, gray and tan—gave way to pastel blue, lavender, pink and electric metallic colors. The change was vivid and abrupt. An obvious corollary was the exciting colors of house interiors. Stoves, refrigerators, toilets and tubs had once been white. By the mid-`50s, they came in mix-and-match colors.

The cover of the August, 1955 *American Home* magazine shows three fashionably-dressed women in a kitchen. The ceiling and cupboard top are white, and the cupboards are pastel blue and the wall behind the women is pink, a combination of colors similar to those found on some 1955-`56 cars.

Articles and ads emphasized the use of color in non-traditional ways. General Electric refrigerator-freezers came in white, but were "available in mix-or-match colors: Canary Yellow, Turquoise Green, Petal Pink, Cadet Blue, Woodtone Brown." Briggs Beautyware bathroom fixtures came in five colors. An ad showed a matching ensemble: pink toilet, bathtub and sink. It was radically different from bathrooms I'd seen where all fixtures were white. A Case plumbing fixtures ad showed a pink toilet and said it was available in "32 decorator colors and sparkling black and white."

The trend was painting walls in at least two colors and doing the trim with a third color. Numerous colors were available, as cited in DuPont Duco and Flow Kote paint ads. Floors also were colorful, with Carnival KenFlex or Pabco "young-at-heart" tiles. Appointments, such as towels, added more color. "What color is your bathroom? No matter! Cannon Carefree Colors will give it new beauty!"

You could mix or match towels and décor. Pink Whisper and New Rose went with pink walls; Marine Blue and Sea green went with green walls.

It's easy to imagine a `50s Chrysler exec, lounging in a tub, looking at the colors in his bathroom and thinking they might look great on a car.

PHILCO 2065 — 20.2 cu. ft.

*Also 14.6 cu. ft. model V-1465 in white,
Startone blue or Suntone yellow.

Painting White Sidewall Tires

In recent months several readers have wondered about the popularity of whitewall tires in the 1940s and 1950s and about the white tire paint used then and if it is available now.

From memory and from era photographs it's clear that cars with whitewall tires (or white sidewall tires) were not often seen. Cost was a factor. In the 1954 Sears' catalogue, the least expensive Allstate 6:70x15 whitewall was $18.35; a comparable blackwall was $10.95, while a "Safti-Cap" (recap) was $9.95. A blackwall tire was approximately half as expensive as a whitewall and if a person were buying four or five tires, that was a considerable difference in price. It could mean spending $40 vs. $80 on a car that might only have cost $100.

Because of the cost, and because of the rubber shortages that went back to World War II, whitewall tires—and especially used whitewall tires— were not as readily available as blackwall tires. Unfortunately, most people seem to have forgotten the economics of the 1950s, when a dollar was a considerable amount of money. It was what most of us got for an hour's work! I do not remember buying even one new tire during the 1950s; for most of the decade I bought used tires, and toward the end I bought recaps. Had there been an abundance of good used whitewalls, reasonably priced, I probably would have bought them.

It was not uncommon to see high buck custom cars with white tires on the front and blackwall tires on the rear. On a lowered car with skirts you couldn't see the sidewalls anyway, so what did it matter? That example (documented in photographs) demonstrates that whitewalls were considered desirable, but that cost and availability were important factors.

In 1952, both my cars had blackwall tires. I had a decent 1939 Mercury convertible, with the original green paint, and it looked okay with black tires. On my Model A roadster I was more concerned with the tire size. I had 7:00x16s on the back and 6:00x16s on the front; the tread pattern was the same on all four tires, which was essential on a car without front fenders. Later I got a pair of 5:50x16 whitewalls for the front and ran blackwalls in back. Not until 1956 did I put a pair of fake whitewalls, called Port-A-Walls, on the back to make things more uniform.

Whitewalls became important to me in 1953, and to others also, it seems, because you began to see more cars with them. In June I bought a clean `37 Ford coupe, which had duals, a new chrome grille, and full wheel covers. It was primer gray and I thought it would look better with whitewalls. Unable to afford new tires for my $45 car, one of the first things I did was to paint the sidewalls white.

Readers have asked if white tire paint is still available. I haven't seen it in stores for years. I can't even find black tire paint anymore! But I did find a kit called White Wall Marvel that probably dates from 1953. It urges, "Do it yourself! Make beautiful white walls of your black tires." To show how easily this could be done, the box shows a woman applying the white material to a blackwall tire. The material is described as "pure white colloidal rubber" that "seals itself permanently to tire walls." A blurb on the box stresses that this is "not a paint or enamel", that it "actually becomes part of the tire" and that it's "safe."

The product did everything it promised, and it was easily cleaned with a hose and rag. But it was less than "permanent", and within weeks it began to check and fade so that the job had to be done again. This was especially true if you'd brushed against a curb. As with any attempt to cover a surface, the later coats looked rough, because you were painting over imperfections. It also helped if you didn't work often, because painting tires became part-time work, like a second job!

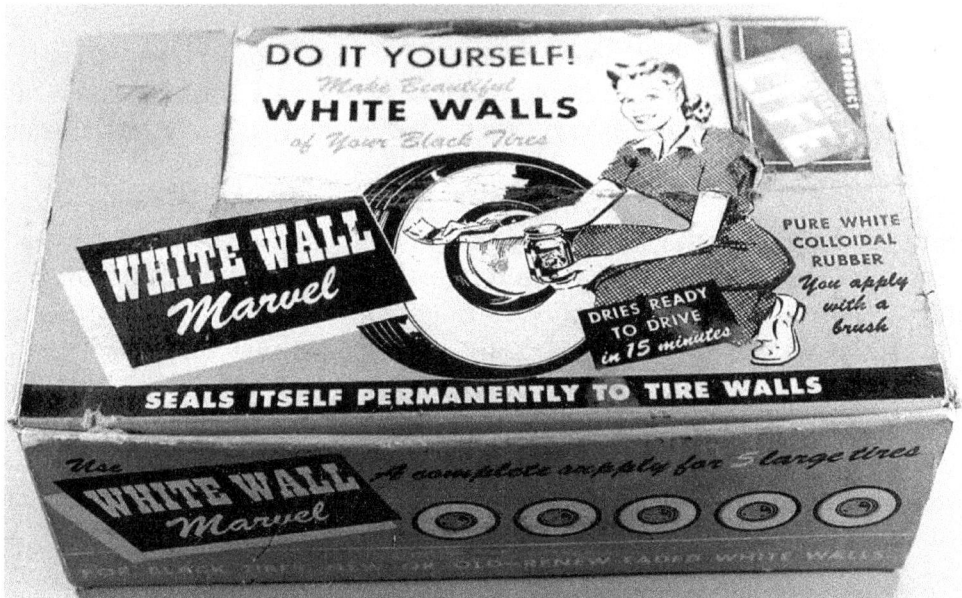

Vittles, Vehicles: American Style

During the holidays, with a traditional dinner of turkey and dressing, mashed potatoes and gravy, sweet potatoes and cranberry sauce, I kept thinking of the phrase "As American as apple pie." It holds an inherent truth I had never considered: the French apple tart and German apple strudel notwithstanding, America is the land of apple pies. I can't think of another country where apple pie is on the menu: in America it has been developed to an art form. On another level it symbolizes what is American: the richness, fullness, the things for which we give thanks.

Perhaps because the pie is round, like a tire or a steering wheel, I associate it with a car—an American car, non-specific, but long, low, something from the 1950s. Such a car, like apple pie, is utterly American: the two go together like—well, bacon and eggs, macaroni and cheese, liver and onions. When such cars were on the road all food was American! Creamed corn beef and cabbage, baked beans and Boston brown bread (in a round can!), beef stew, prune whip, hamburger in various forms—patties, meatloaf, meatballs; deviled ham, Spam, chili, frankfurters, Birds Eye frozen vegetables, cole slaw.

We drove cars made in America, and ate food grown in America! Corn on the cob, potato salad. Pineapple was exotic, as were Spanish green olives with a bright red pimento in each center. Even canned fruit cocktail seemed exotic.

Our diet was home-grown but not bland nor limited. No one tired of a really good hamburger, even if it was made with packaged white bread, and a cheeseburger was heavenly. A good restaurant that served breaded veal cutlets, chicken-fried steak, a chop or beefsteak was always busy; you could identify them by the rows of American cars in the parking lot.

Was it a coincidence that chains like Taco Bell and Taco Time opened eateries about the time foreign cars began to arrive by the boatload? When the streets were jammed with Toyotas and Nissans gas stations closed right and left, to open their doors to Asian eateries. An occasional NYC expatriate cried that he could not find a decent bagel. What is a bagel? I wondered. What is lox?

Along the way traditions were lost. The holiday turkey dinner is one that remains, and I suppose a guy can still enjoy it, even if he drives, say, a BMW.

1953 Cadillac Le Mans

It is a natural condition that things are always in transition. But sometimes the transitional period is more emphatic than other times. That was true of automobiles during the mid-'50s. Seemingly overnight car bodies became streamlined and by 1955 nearly every car line had gotten rid of its antique engine in favor of the modern, overhead-valve V-8. Cars got lower, sleeker, faster, grew fins, and boasted all kinds of gizmos. These trends and devices were most evident in the various factory "dream" cars.

In 1953 Cadillac toured the nation with its new Le Mans "experimental custom," and there was great excitement when it came to Portland, Oregon in November for a three day showing. It was billed as an "experimental custom sports car." There was enormous interest in sports cars, but they were rare at that time in the Portland area and every red-blooded car guy jumped at the chance to see one. We were also aware of the two Cadillacs—one a stock-bodied two-door hardtop—that Briggs Cunningham had raced at the 24 hours of Le Mans just three years earlier when we had speculated as to how well that factory car might perform. When the dust finally settled, the two Cadillacs had finished 10th and 11th overall! Cadillac had no doubt chosen the name Le Mans knowing that something of Cunningham's success would carry over to this car.

Although we were reluctant to call the Le Mans a sports car—we had the same opinion about the new Corvette and Thunderbird when they came out—it was a neat job. It was nearly eight inches lower than the '53 Cadillac Series 62 convertible and several inches shorter. It carried only three people and the body was made of "plastic fiberglass." I can't recall whether I had heard of that new material, but I know I had never seen a fiberglass car. With a 250-hp engine, equipped with dual four-barrel carburetors, the car looked fast. Even the engine had been painted Le Mans Blue to match the exterior of the car.

It had features that we knew we wouldn't find on a true sports car, but they interested us. The blue leather interior, for example, at the forward edge of the seat had a tube containing an umbrella! The seat itself had a "memory"; it automatically slid back when the door was opened, then returned to its former position when the door closed. Another feature of interest was the top, which automatically slid into the rear deck when recessed. If it began to rain while the vehicle was unattended with the top down, it automatically came up when a "rain switch" was activated. Devices like these convinced us we were, in fact, seeing the car of the future.

I have since learned that Cadillac probably built four examples of the Le Mans. One was owned by Harry Karl, the late husband of Debbie Reynolds. While hard to believe today, at some point that one was customized by George Barris! However, it was eventually destroyed in a fire. Two others remain privately owned, while the fourth example's fate is unclear.

CADILLAC BARNARD'S OLDSMOBILE SERVICE BULLETIN

21st & WEST BURNSIDE . . . ATwater 6241

NOVEMBER, 1953 — PUBLISHED IN YOUR INTEREST FOR SAFER, MORE COMFORTABLE DRIVING

SPECIAL 3-DAY SHOWING OF FAMOUS "LE MANS" CADILLAC

Sensational experimental custom sports car with sleek, plastic fibreglass body, 250 H.P. and other features to be on display

BARNARD'S SHOWROOM — THURSDAY, NOVEMBER 19th THROUGH
SATURDAY, NOVEMBER 21st, 8 A.M. TO 5 P.M.

WINTER CAR-SAVING CHECK LIST

LUBRICATION:
Winter grade oil and grease in
☐ motor ☐ transmission ☐ chassis
☐ differential ☐ oil filter change

COOLING SYSTEM
Check condition:
☐ radiator hose ☐ heater hose
☐ fan belt
☐ Leaks at gaskets, pumps, hose clamp
☐ Thermostat operation
☐ System ready for NEW anti-freeze?

MOTOR CONDITION:
If you want to know exactly the condition of your motor, we suggest
☐ Thoro-check — 60 instrument tests
☐ Check battery ☐ Check spark plugs ☐ Major tune-up ☐ Minor tune-up

SAFETY-CHECK:
☐ Brakes adjusted ☐ Brake fluid
☐ Wheel alignment ☐ Chains
☐ Tires balanced ☐ Lights ☐ Squirts
☐ Windshield ☐ Swipe blades

APPEARANCE AND FINISH:
The easiest way to protect your car's finish against winter weather is a complete BLUE CORAL treatment.

Remember, our Courtesy Car, on the hour and half-hour for your convenience.

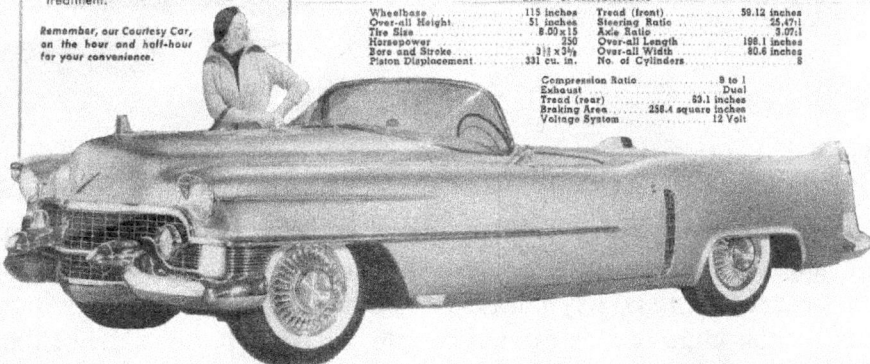

The Le Mans

With the present high public interest in sports type cars, Cadillac's experimental custom Le Mans will fascinate Portland viewers with its racy, sleek line. Its plastic fibreglass body and many advanced features. Powered with a Cadillac V-8 engine stepped up to deliver 250 horsepower with a 9-1 compression ratio, this three-passenger convertible combines speed, power and roadability. Among its numerous mechanical refinements are two four-barrel carburetors, redesigned manifolds, high-lift valves, two special air cleaners and mufflers. Its HydraMatic transmission, as well as other friction points, have been adapted to the higher engine performance. The engine itself is painted to match the exclusive Le Mans blue color of the car.

The Le Mans is 51 inches high at the top of the panoramic pillar windshield, 7.9 inches lower than the standard Cadillac convertible. Its overall length of 196.1 inches is shorter than the standard Cadillac, part of which is accounted for by unique rear bumpers which are vertical strips of steel, rather than the conventional horizontal bar, and appear to be part of the body. However, they are internally braced and capable of withstanding shock as well as other more familiar bumper.

Another unique feature of this car is the "memory" seat. Electrically controlled, it automatically slides back as the door is opened to provide easier access and egress. When the door is closed, it "remembers" its former position and returns to it. The seat is, of course, also adjustable to the comfort of the driver.

Upholstery of the Le Mans is of finest hand-buffed leather of a matching blue color and embossed in the leather at the center of the seat backrest is the Cadillac crest. The bolster at the forward edge of the seat contains a tube for umbrella storage. The tube has a chromed cap carrying the Le Mans in-

signia and when the cap is removed the umbrella is pushed out by an injector spring for easy grasping.

Carpeting is of nylon needlepoint and heel pads are of leather stripped with chrome. The entire interior is chrome trimmed and door hardware is of the pushbutton type.

The unusual instrument panel features matching circular dials extending the width of the board, including a tachometer to show engine revolutions, a speedometer, fuel gauge, radio dial, ammeter and oil pressure gauge and clock. Twin radio speakers are recessed behind the panel while the HydraMatic indicator has been moved from the customary place on the steering post and customized into the instrument panel between the tachometer and speedometer. Lights, lighter, and radio control knobs are formed of harmonizing, luminescent plastic, while heater and ventilating controls are airplane-type levers. The entire panel is topped with a pad insulated with a special, slow-recovery plastic which tends to eliminate the rebound found in rubber.

The top of the Le Mans is of white orlon and, when lowered, automatically recesses into the rear deck. In addition to the regular switch, the top is also actuated by a rain switch to provide automatic raising if the car is left out and a shower occurs.

The wheels of this special convertible represent a further advance over the wire wheels which are currently enjoying a revival on sports cars. Instead of wire spokes, these have chromed blades inspired by the blades of an aircraft turbine. Besides offering unusual attractiveness, these bladed wheels provide superior cooling for the car's power brakes.

Other interesting features of this car include headlight shields formed by extensions of the front fenders, license plate holder covered with clear plastic and placed flush with the bumpers, and sponge plastic armrests built into the body and harmonizing completely with the metallic blue color of the car.

BRIEF SPECIFICATIONS

Wheelbase	115 inches	Tread (front)	59.12 inches
Over-all Height	51 inches	Steering Ratio	25.47:1
Tire Size	8.00 x 15	Axle Ratio	3.07:1
Horsepower	250	Over-all Length	196.1 inches
Bore and Stroke	3⅞ x 3⅜	Over-all Width	80.6 inches
Piston Displacement	331 cu. in.	No. of Cylinders	8
		Compression Ratio	9 to 1
		Exhaust	Dual
		Tread (rear)	63.1 inches
		Braking Area	258.4 square inches
		Voltage System	12 Volt

REMEMBER: ONLY 3 DAYS — NOVEMBER 19TH THROUGH NOVEMBER 21ST TO SEE THIS CAR OF THE FUTURE

Independence

When WW II ended, a weight was lifted and there was a great sense of optimism. Servicemen returned home and many headed for college under the GI Bill. Factories were converted to peacetime, and began turning out new automobiles, toasters, vacuum cleaners and all those other necessary products. New inventions, such as television, were right around the corner. Thousands of houses were being built. Radio quiz shows abounded, like "64 Dollar Question", "It Pays to be Ignorant" and "Queen for a Day", shows that gave away money to just about everyone.

In those optimistic days after the war ended, my father could not simply go to work for someone else; he was determined to be his own boss. My mother made a simple distinction: there were blue collar workers and white collar workers, and she urged him to become one of the latter. He could sell appliances, real estate or used cars. For once, she had the right idea, but my father had made good money during the war and he knew there was lots more to be made.

He decided to start his own excavation business. He teamed up with a fellow who had been a welder in the ship yards, and together they borrowed money to buy some equipment: a used gasoline shovel with a back hoe, an ancient steam shovel, a bulldozer and a couple beat-up dump trucks. These machines were man-killers. My father worked hard, always kept busy digging basements for the huge homes of rich people in Oswego, but I doubt that he ever made much money. The machines constantly let him down. He was always working on them, often in the rain, doing something to the bulldozer's blade or the shovel's track, using hydraulic jacks, wooden blocks, long steel pry bars and a sledge hammer. He was not a big man, and it must have taken something out of him every time he swung that hammer.

Where Did You Go? Out. What Did You Do? Nothing.

Out of high school, waiting to be drafted, this is how they spent the time after work and before sleep. They parked behind the service station, stood around, kicked a tire, traded lies, postured, day-dreamed, dangled in time.

After dinner they left their respective houses, drove separate streets through traffic so sparse it was no problem. Each had washed his car, whether painted or primered, scrubbed the whitewalls with bleach or an SOS pad, swept the front floor with a whisk broom. The dash smelled of car wax, and the small green tree hung under the dash, in front of the heater, permeated the car with the odor of fresh pine. Although the car might be old, everything about it seemed clean and fresh, and even the heavy sweet odor of blowby had a freshness about it.

They drove on separate streets, cruising easily, the sound of duals barely building behind the car. On main streets the driver slowed to check the reflection of his car in large store windows: the paint, whitewalls, hubcaps. The general picture was enough to please him; at a distance any imperfections did not exist.

They came together at the Mobil station, each downshifting half a block away, the duals richly backing off, and they parked behind the station. Jim's `40 Ford Deluxe coupe, primered, blacked out, a Lincoln-Zephyr front bumper, and a new Merc flathead for street and strip. Al's almost new 1949 Ford business coupe, black, lowered, nosed and decked, a 1949 Chevy license plate guard on the rear bumper and dual pipes. Norm's 1940 Mercury convertible, gray primer, new white top, and serious duals.

They got out, leaned on cars, stood around, smoking, talking about what they'd done and what they planned to do. Because you could not have a smooth car without being smooth, each guy had had a recent haircut and had shaved. They wore pegged sun tans or bright white cords, nicely pressed, a sharp shirt, and shoes polished until a guy could see his reflection.

Why have a chromed and polished engine if you were not equally sharp? Why have rolled and pleated Naugahyde upholstery if you wore greasy clothes? Because it made sense to be at least as tidy as your car these guys were always well turned-out, with a narrow belt, the belt-loops sewn across so that the belt fit in the lower half, argyle socks, thin cuffs on their pants. To dress in this manner, to pay attention to your clothes, hair, and shoes, was as important as having a sharp car, and it all came together to define the meaning of "smooth."

You had to be sharp, even if you were simply hanging out behind a service station. And for a period of time this was what young men did, in the years between high school and starting a family. It was a ritual that took place all over the nation. What else could they do, or where could they go? TV was virtually nonexistent and, anyway, there was little to watch. Fast food was not even a concept then. Yes, they could go to a drive-in restaurant, and later often did. When older, they would meet at a tavern, but they did not forsake the ritual of meeting at a service station to discuss things.

Years later, after a family or families, marriages and divorces, wars and recessions, jobs good and bad, diseases and deaths, they would recall the years almost beyond memory, and a time when a chunk of life was given over to standing beside a car behind a gas station.

What did we do? they'd ask. Nothing worth mentioning.

The obvious question then is: how could it have been so much fun?

Hulks

Once upon a time, when the world was younger, people found machines in vacant fields, behind barns, in the trees that formed a windbreak about a farm or a hundred other places. For the children who found the machines they were space ships, sailing ships, covered wagons or airplanes, but most often they were race cars that had come to rest in this empty place.

The boy approached through browned grass that was as tall as his nose. A grasshopper clacked in summer heat, and a yellow and black spider larger than a 50-cent piece danced around the fly captured in the silk web. In the heat the ripe grass smelled like baked bread. Above the tops of the grass, he could see an angular shape, like a lop-sided cabin, and as he got closer he saw that it was a machine, the weathered metal two shades darker than the brown grass around him. He wondered how long it had been here, angled to the ground as if it had crashed.

No house was nearby, therefore no one owned the car, so he climbed onto the runningboard and looked through the broken window. The seats were split, and cotton showed at every seam. The wheel that had steered the machine to this place to this empty field at the edge of the city, had blackened, but on its rim was a red knob, like a jewel. He pulled on the ornate door handle, as hard as he could, but the door would not budge.

Slowly he circled the machine, beating down the tall grass, wary of snakes. A hubcap lay on the ground and from it a green lizard jumped. The boy climbed onto the passenger side runningboard and found this door ajar; even so, it took all his strength to push it open a few inches, as if he were opening an airlock or a crypt. The heat spun out, musty with the overwhelming odor of old grease. He waited, listening for the hum of a bee or a hornet; wary too of the field mice which must live in the seats. He reached his hand out toward the jewel.

What characterized the moment was the absolute silence. There was no traffic noise, nor human sounds, such as a mother calling a child, not even an insect sound nor the wisp of grass brushing against metal in the breeze. He was totally alone in this world, in this space. He climbed onto the front seat, and pulled at the knob, which refused to come off. Then he rocked the wheel, an imitation of steering, and looked through the crazed, yellowed glass of the windshield. The endless field ahead became a road, and when a curve appeared he romped on the wheel, reached or the gear shift, wished that his feet could meet the pedals.

Before he left he unscrewed the gear shift knob and carefully reached under the seat, fearful of spiders, snakes and field mice, where he found a radiator ornament and beat-up license plate. These he carried home and put on a shelf in his room. Before summer ended he returned with two friends, and they brought a hammer and a hacksaw. They got the red squirrel knob off by sawing a section from the wheel; also a taillight, and the ID plate from the firewall. Then the machine became a bomber, and for the rest of the afternoon the three young pilots fought the Axis powers.

Years later, when he hunted rabbits in the field, he saw that the car was still there, the grass around it higher, a few more parts missing. Someone had jumped on the hood, and the top fabric flapped in the breeze. Three bullet holes had pierced the body in back, and as he left he pumped a bullet into the hulk, for the heck of it.

Later still, he went away to the state college, and when he returned for Christmas vacation he realized that a rough road had been cut across the field; it was too muddy to drive on, and from a distance he could not see the ancient, angled car.

When he next returned, at the beginning of summer, dozens of houses had been built in the vacant field, cars moved quickly along the new road, and drivers honked as he slowed near the place where he guessed the old car might have been, now the site of a 7-11. Back home, he found the red jewel of a squirrel knob in his old room and after cleaning it up, he clamped it to the steering wheel of his fairly-new, but otherwise uninteresting, sedan.

AUTOMOBILE INSTALLMENT NOTE   NO. 6120

$ 845.76   Portland,   , Oregon,   Feb. 21,   , 19 41

FOR VALUE RECEIVED, I promise to pay to the order of THE FIRST NATIONAL BANK OF PORTLAND, at its Southeast Portland Branch, in the City of Portland   , Oregon, the sum of Eight hundred forty five and 76/100------------------ DOLLARS, in   24   equal and successive monthly installments of not less than   Thirty five and 24/100----------------------- DOLLARS ($ 35.24   ) in any one payment. The first installment shall be paid on the   21   day of   March   , 19 41 , and a like installment shall be paid on the   21st   day of each month thereafter until   3/5/43 , at which time the full balance then owing shall be paid. If any of said installments are not so paid at the time and in the manner herein provided, the whole sum then owing shall become, at the option of the holder of this note, immediately due and payable. If default occurs in the payment of any of said installments, I promise to pay interest upon such installment or installments at the rate of eight per cent per annum from the date upon which the same shall have become due until paid. In case suit or action is instituted to collect this note, or any portion thereof, I promise to pay such additional sum as the Court may adjudge reasonable as attorney's fees in said suit or action. The endorsers, guarantors and sureties hereon severally waive presentment for payment, demand, notice of dishonor, protest and notice of protest.

Telephone   *Albert H Drake*

Address   9727 S. E. Reedway

N-348 ORE. 3-40

About the Author

Albert Drake was born in Portland, Oregon when it was less populous and life had the quality of Norman Rockwell paintings. He was educated in public schools and followed his father's footsteps, working for years in service stations, garages and automotive warehouses. He eventually attended Portland State College, and got his degrees at the University of Oregon. He twice won the Ernest Haycox Prize for fiction. For nearly 30 years he labored in the groves of academe, where he was cited for his outstanding teaching and rose to the rank of Full Professor. He was the first academic to teach a class in science fiction as literature, and for several years he was Director of the Clarion Science Fiction Workshop. He has received numerous academic and creative grants, including two major grants from the National Endowment for the Arts. His fiction, poetry and prose have been widely published in literary quarterlies and popular magazines, including *Redbook*, *Epoch*, *North American Review* and *The Best American Short Stories*. He is currently Professor Emeritus of English.

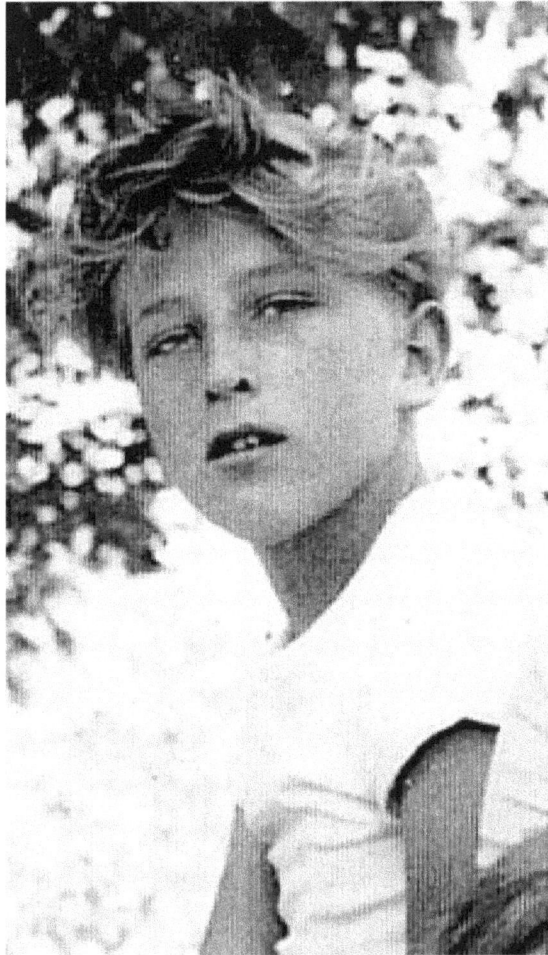

Albert Drake
(August 1, 1948)

www.ingramcontent.com/pod-product-compliance
Lightning Source LLC
Chambersburg PA
CBHW080516110426
42742CB00017B/3140